SUSTAINING ENVIRONMENTAL MANAGEMENT SUCCESS

Wiley Quality Management Series

Sustaining Environmental Management Success: Best Business Practices from Industry Leaders
(0-471-24645-X)
by W. Gary Wilson and Dennis R. Sasseville

ISO 14000: The Business Manager's Complete Guide to Environmental Management
(0-471-16564-6)
by Perry Johnson

QS-9000 Answer Book: 101 Questions & Answers About the Automotive Quality System Standard
(0-471-15700-7)
by Rob Kanter

ISO 14000 Answer Book: Environmental Management for the World Market
(0-471-17933-7)
by Dennis R. Sasseville, W. Gary Wilson and Robert Lawson

SUSTAINING ENVIRONMENTAL MANAGEMENT SUCCESS

Best Business Practices from Industry Leaders

W. GARY WILSON
DENNIS R. SASSEVILLE

3 1336 04766 9677

JOHN WILEY & SONS

New York ■ Chichester ■ Weinheim ■ Brisbane ■ Singapore ■ Toronto

Copyright © 1999 by W. Gary Wilson & Dennis R. Sasseville. All rights reserved.
Published by John Wiley & Sons, Inc.
Published simultaneously in Canada.

This publication is designed to provide accurate and authoritative information in
regard to the subject matter covered. It is sold with the understanding that the
publisher is not engaged in rendering legal, accounting, or other professional
services. If legal advice or other expert assistance is required, the services of a
competent professional person should be sought.

Library of Congress Cataloging-in-Publication Data:

Wilson, W. Gary, 1948–
    Sustaining environmental management success:
  best business practices from industry leaders / Dennis R. Sasseville, W. Gary Wilson.
      p.   cm. — (Wiley quality management series)
    Includes index.
    ISBN 0-471-24645-X (cloth : alk. paper)
    1. Industrial management—Environmental aspects.   2. Environmental
  management.   3. Business enterprises—Environmental aspects.
  I. Wilson, W. Gary, 1948–   . II. Title. III. Series.
  HD30.255.S27   1998
  658.4′08—dc21   98-17661
                                                                      CIP

Printed in the United States of America.

10 9 8 7 6 5 4 3 2 1

With love, to Joanna, whose support made the hours of research and writing possible, and to my grandchildren, Dakotah, Canyon, Ashleigh, and those yet unborn, for whom the reality of sustainability will be much more than an abstract concept.

W. GARY WILSON

My efforts in developing and writing this book could not have been possible without the unfailing dedication and love of my wife, Kathy, and my daughters, Erin and Renee. Thank you for tolerating my long hours of seclusion in researching and writing this work. It is dedicated to the three of you who are all very special to me. I also thank my parents, parents-in-law, and my extended family of New Hampshire friends for their support.

DENNIS R. SASSEVILLE

FOREWORD

In recent years, there has been a marked shift in people's attitudes toward environmental protection. It has become part of our consciousness, institutionalized in our society. People have come to expect it.

A similar transformation is taking place in industry and business. At most companies, it is no longer a question of *if* they will comply with environmental regulations. That's a given. Leading companies, however, are going even farther. We now are asking ourselves how we can more closely align our environmental practices with our business strategy in order to make the best decisions for our companies.

Environmental management clearly has entered a new phase. This is an outgrowth of the recognition that environmental protection and economic progress are not mutually exclusive—that there is a way to protect the environment but at the same time use our resources sustainably to provide necessary goods.

Gary Wilson and Dennis Sasseville have written a book that takes a closer look at this new approach to environmental management. They have identified companies that are leading the way in incorporating environmental considerations into every aspect of how they do business.

They also provide a helpful, in-depth discussion of how an environmental management system works and what it takes to implement one successfully.

All of us who work in businesses with environmental impacts understand that integrating a company's environmental practices with its business strategy takes a strong commitment at all levels of the organization. That commitment is built on a shared belief that environmental protection matters, that it's the right thing to do.

The authors go a step further and show how this new approach to environmental management makes good business sense as well—that smart environmental management *can* add value.

The cost-competitive global business environment in which we operate today tempts us to focus on short-term gains. Leading companies know that environmental protection is a long-term responsibility. Achieving a balance between economic considerations and environmental responsibilities is what the new approach to environmental management is all about. This book provides a helpful guide to finding the way.

A.D. "Pete" Correll
Chairman and Chief Executive Officer
Georgia-Pacific Corporation
Atlanta, Georgia
April 1998

ACKNOWLEDGMENTS

The authors thank the many professional colleagues and clients from both industry and consulting for sharing their experiences in environmental and EHS management issues. We also benefited greatly from discussions with our many colleagues at QST Environmental and KPMG Peat Marwick, LLP, and thank them for sharing ideas and insights that helped shape this project.

The authors also acknowledge the assistance of Nicholas Smith and Andrea Pedolsky at the Altair Literary Agency for their advice and guidance on this project, and Susan Malette at Digital Equipment Corporation for sharing her insights into quality principles and relationships to ISO 14000.

We are especially indebted to Jim Morash for his excellent editing services and numerous helpful suggestions in preparing the manuscript.

CONTENTS

CONTENTS

CONTENTS

Section III Integration and the Road to Value-Based Management

INTRODUCTION

This book is written for both business and environmental professionals who have tried to sort out the new trends with environmental management and environmental management systems (EMS). Some of you feel you have heard too much hype, or have been to one too many ISO 14000 seminars and still have questions such as: What does it all mean for me and my company? How do I learn more about the companies that are finding success with their environmental management initiatives? This book was written to answer these types of questions.

Today, companies around the world are making cultural changes in how they approach their operations' interactions with the environment, in their understanding of these environmental impacts, and in their relationships with regulatory agencies and interested parties. This book was researched and written to provide the reader with an understanding of the issues of environmental management and its relationship to sustainability and value-based management, by looking at what leading companies are actually doing. Real-world examples abound: How a company has, for example, written an environmental policy, identified its environmental aspects, integrated business goals with environmental management, achieved a start at sustainability, or integrated quality and EHS initiatives. (Note that we use *environmental management* and *environmental, health, and safety management* interchangeably throughout this text.)

The book extensively discusses EMS concepts and the natural link to ISO 14001 and the related ISO 14000 series standards. The growing global acceptance of ISO 14001 as *the* EMS cannot and should not be ignored. If you are planning an EMS for your company it just makes sense to seriously consider ISO 14001 (or ISO 14004, which provides general guidance on EMS) as the framework. Certification to ISO 14001, however, is a completely separate consideration. Most, if not all, companies can benefit from an EMS patterned after ISO 14001; however, only a subset of these companies will, or perhaps

INTRODUCTION

should, seek third-party certification of their EMS. Companies considering certification need to look at a whole host of potential driving forces, including market and customer demands, industry sector competition, regulatory agency incentives or dictates, and so forth. So, we do not dwell on ISO 14001 as an end point, but our discussions about EMS are clearly rooted in the ISO 14001 model.

In researching best EHS practices for the book, we looked at many companies, but this was not undertaken as a survey-ranking approach. Likewise, we have not tried to portray these highlighted companies as necessarily the best at all aspects of environmental management. Many other companies have made great strides toward innovative environmental management, and their stories have been profiled in other environmental texts. The companies that are highlighted in this text were chosen because they provide good examples of particular elements of successful environmental management, business and environmental integration, sustainability, or EMS implementation. We hope that you the reader, learn from some of these best business practices and use those that best fit your needs and situation. There are abundant examples to choose from.

The companies highlighted in this book are some of the first to seriously embrace the concept of systematic integrated environmental management. They are progressive in their approaches and are the early leaders in demonstrating the benefits of going beyond regulatory compliance. Why have they been so progressive? Because it is good for business. It is also good for the environment. But a company must first look to what sustains the business, for without a healthy business everything else falls away. These companies have realized that good business and environmental management are not at odds (as has seemed the case during 25-plus years of command-and-control environmental regulations), but are in fact synergistic. That is, proactive environmental management creates opportunities, avoids liabilities, is more cost-effective, and results in long-term improvements in how a company interacts with the environment. In short, environmental management is good for business and these successful companies know it.

The book, therefore, also looks at environmental reporting and links to financial accounting. More and more, companies are being evaluated for their environmental performance as well as their financial performance. Banks and investors are recognizing the influence of environmental performance (good or bad) on a company's bottom line. Insurance companies are considering whether environmental performance can be used as an indicator of a company's potential risks for underwriting policies. Companies adopting an EMS approach may or may not bring about radical change in the banking or insurance businesses any time soon. Nevertheless, improved environmental performance is being talked about, people are thinking about it, and wherever this trend leads, progressive companies will have changed the way environmental issues are formed, addressed, and resolved.

In response to internal and external drivers, companies are beginning to track environmental costs differently. For years, environmental costs were narrowly viewed as specific costs of doing business, including environmental staff labor costs, control equipment costs, treatment facilities costs, disposal costs, administrative costs associated with meeting regulatory requirements, and fines and penalties. Secondary costs, such as those associated with product marketability, investor confidence, insurance, or competitiveness, have been largely ignored or, at best, misunderstood. Likewise, potential secondary cost savings associated with environmentally friendly design, product stewardship, pollution prevention, or recycling and reuse have not always received due consideration from skeptical controllers and plant managers.

No longer can a company afford to look at environmental costs as only the cost of maintaining regulatory compliance. Environmental performance has an impact on all aspects of a company's operations, whether it be investment rating, insurability, ability to compete, or environmental regulatory compliance. Progressive companies have made significant effort toward tracking all of the impacts, positive and negative, of their environmental performance. These companies have begun to understand and measure how environmental performance affects their ability to get favorable financing, the value of green products to gaining a competitive edge, the cost savings associated with pollution prevention, or the cost savings associated with better control of nonregulated resources (e.g., energy use, water use, and paper recycling).

We talk early in the book about sustainability and sustainable production. EMS is largely an outgrowth of the realization in the late 1980s and early 1990s that continued industrialization around the world will require a different approach to how we use the earth's resources. The Brundtland Commission (World Commission on Environment and Development, 1987) and the Rio Earth Summit (U.N. Conference on Environment and Development, 1992)

INTRODUCTION

provided the catalyst for international standardization in environmental management. The interest in EMS as an international standard of the International Organization for Standardization (ISO) was sparked by the Brundtland Commission Report, and the formation of the Strategic Advisory Group on the Environment by ISO in 1991 was in anticipation of the Rio Earth Summit.

Therefore, the sustainability debate forms a foundation for the entire discussion of systematic environmental management. It speaks to the need to find ways to use and reuse resources more effectively and to make products that are environmentally friendly from "cradle to grave"; that is, during production, during use, and at the end of their intended use. A sustainability approach to environmental performance is much different from regulatory compliance. Sustainable production is at its core a resource issue. Unlike environmental regulations, sustainable production doesn't start with output impacts. It addresses other environmental impacts (i.e., emissions, waste disposal, etc.) by recognizing that the earth can accept a finite amount of refuse and, therefore, that sustainable production must address both inputs and outputs. It addresses these issues by taking a holistic look at a company's impacts.

The central tenet of EMS is the notion of environmental aspects: How does your company interact with the environment? The remainder of the EMS process flows from this determination of environmental aspects. It is because of the developing notion of sustainability that EMS is structured in that way, and that is why EMS presents such a cultural change for most companies. Likewise, the EMS provides a mechanism to create and maintain environmental awareness, to identify opportunities, to track and control our efforts to mitigate environmental impacts, to create better operational processes, and to monitor, review, and improve. An EMS is, therefore, a tool that can be used to achieve sustainability.

We have structured this book to help you follow a natural progression of these changes in the way you manage your company's environmental issues. The book has three major parts, each with a general theme. Section I, "The Foundation," establishes a basis for the birth of EMS, identifies the driving forces behind the interest in voluntary environmental improvements, looks at where environmental management is headed, and describes how progressive companies have established forward-looking visions and policies relative to environmental management. Section II, "The EMS Approach," looks in detail at the systems approach, including the basic structure of an EMS, how companies plan and implement an EMS, certification considerations, and how companies are taking more aggressive roles in measuring and reporting their environmental performance. Section III, "Integration and the Road to Value-Based Management," looks at how companies are taking these new concepts and integrating them into their mainstream business strategies and how that integration leads to overall value creation for the company.

So, there is nothing left to do but to start. Whether your company is committed to developing a more formal EMS, is just testing the waters of environmental accounting, or is seeking EMS certification, we think you will find this book a valuable resource. We hope it broadens your understanding of the origins, the nature, and the future of EHS management. Take the best business practices and experiences we have highlighted and make them your own. Best of luck.

SECTION I

THE FOUNDATION

The first three chapters of this book, grouped together as they are, purposely lay a foundation. They serve as an expanded introduction, setting the tone and framework for understanding the evolution of the formalized Environmental Management System (EMS) and the associated best practices among leading companies in North America and the global community. Sections II and III will explore in greater detail the critical components of EMS initiatives and discuss some of the significant trends in environmental accounting, in performance measurement and reporting, and in addressing the concerns of the stakeholder—the ultimate driver for quality, business, and environmental improvements.

ON THE ROAD TO SUSTAINABILITY THROUGH ENVIRONMENTAL MANAGEMENT

Sustainable development suggests a balance among the environment, the economy and social equity. It challenges us to find approaches to business which provide robust, long-term health for the environment, for the individual, for local economies and for the business itself.

EH&S PERFORMANCE REPORT—1997
BAXTER INTERNATIONAL

In one sense, environmental management has been practiced since the beginning of the organized enterprise. Even in the occupations of early Egypt or other pre–Christian era civilizations, the business owner had to give thought to the source of resources or the disposal of wastes, although in a world still ripe with natural resources and largely untouched by the debris of human activity, environmental management was never *consciously* considered. It would be several thousand years before humankind needed to give serious thought to the notions of environmental impact and management of resources.

Certainly in the twentieth century, companies have been aware of their interaction with the environment within which they conduct their business. Until the late 1960s and early 1970s, however, many companies frequently misunderstood or ignored the impact of their operation on that environment. The capacity for the earth to provide resources and to accept our waste seemed infinite. However, the industrial revolution was straining that global capacity. By the 1970s, rivers were dying, the Rhine was on fire, Lake Erie was all but dead, and the air was becoming unbreathable in many urban areas. In the United States, that all began to change with the advent of congressional activities and publicly expressed concerns for the environmental impact resulting from our industrialized society.

Most often referred to as *command-and-control* regulations, environmental laws began to prescribe how a company should manage its impact on selected parts of the environment. We say *selected parts* because environmental regulations had not addressed issues of resource consumption, nor directly addressed such issues as biodiversity, land use, and population. Nevertheless, command-and-control regulations had resulted in significant reductions in pollutant emissions. Environmental management had come of age and awareness of environmental impacts, at least those that were regulated, became a reality.

In the late 1980s, a new concept evolved that would question the manner in which we viewed environmental management. This was the concept of *sustainable development*, a phrase that was introduced by the 1987 report of the World Commission on Environment and Development (the Brundtland Commission), *Our Common Future.* It was this notion of *sustainability* that led to the current awareness and interest in environmental management systems and other nontraditional approaches to managing environmental impacts.[1] An environmental management system (EMS) as we know it today is fundamentally different from the type of reactive or ad hoc environmental management practiced in the past. Although it can incorporate many of the systems used to address regulatory compliance, an EMS requires a change in mind-set. In other words, promulgating an effective EMS requires a cultural change throughout a company. To better understand the concept of EMS it is helpful, if not critical, to understand the concept of sustainability. Likewise, to understand why major corporations have voluntarily developed alternative approaches to environmental management in order to achieve sustainability, it is necessary to understand the driving forces behind sustainable development.

1.1 Sustainable Development

The Brundtland Commission's definition of sustainable development—development that meets the needs of the present without compromising the ability of future generations to meet their own needs—is the one most widely used. The concept of sustainable development received worldwide attention as a result of the United Nations Conference on Environment and Development

("Earth Summit"), held on June 3 to 14, 1992, in Rio de Janeiro, Brazil. A significant outcome of the Earth Summit was the adoption of Agenda 21; this set of guiding principles (Rio Principles; see Appendix D) for achieving sustainability was adopted by 172 nations attending the conference.

Rio Principle 1: Human beings are at the center of concerns for sustainable development. They are entitled to a healthy and productive life in harmony with nature.

Rio Principle 3: The right to development must be fulfilled so as to equitably meet developmental and environmental needs of present and future generations.

The global concern for sustainable development results from a recognition that the predictions are dire for future global conditions, absent some change in our approach to economic growth. Continuing maintenance and growth of developed economies, coupled with the rapid increase in development of emerging countries, consumes ever-increasing quantities of natural and renewable resources. It has become clear that the planet cannot support the rate of resource consumption necessary to meet the economic needs of the world's population without a managed approach to resource use. Increased economic growth also results in increased waste burdens on the planet. Recent data on the ozone layer and the oceans indicate that we are exceeding the capacity of the planet to absorb the current burden, let alone future increased levels.

Rio Principle 8: To achieve sustainable development and a higher quality of life for all people, States should reduce and eliminate unsustainable patterns of production and consumption and promote appropriate demographic policies.

In short, humankind's activities currently are not sustainable into the future. Therefore, two options exist: Continue unsustainable growth and accept a future society that cannot support the world's population, or develop means to achieve growth and development in a manner that is inherently sustainable.

1.2   Characteristics of Leadership Companies

Many large companies were represented at the Earth Summit, companies that have taken an early lead in tackling the issues on the road to sustainable development. Frank Popoff, CEO of Dow Chemical Company, stated in his remarks at the conference that the 1970s was the decade of denial, the 1980s the decade of data, and the 1990s the decade of dialogue with the public. As discussed in the following, many companies have embraced the concept of sustainable development as the only sensible way to do business.

Professor Stuart Hart makes a strong case for corporations being the appropriate entities to take the lead in achieving sustainable development (Hart, 1997). Hart notes that although the root causes against sustainability (e.g., overpopulation, economic development in emerging countries, conflicting priorities between survival concerns and environmental concerns) are certainly social and political issues, only corporations have the financial resources, technical expertise, and infrastructure to develop solutions and alternatives that will lead to sustainability. In an interesting juxtaposition, Professor Hart points out that from a negative viewpoint, corporations may face a world where poverty, degraded environment, and crumbling political systems make doing business increasingly difficult; while from a positive viewpoint, corporations may find that the drive toward sustainability can provide them with innovative and financially advantageous ways of doing business. Either viewpoint makes a compelling case for corporations to take the issues of sustainability seriously.

Companies that take a short-term view of the environment are far more likely to design projects that adversely affect the natural resource base, thereby incurring negative media attention, regulatory penalties and other disciplinary measures, as well as public displeasure, each of which potentially creates long-term impediments to business success.

Grace Wever, Ph.D.
KPMG Environmental Management Practice

What kinds of companies have taken the lead in EMS and sustainable development? There is no single demographic; all sizes and types of companies have developed appropriate environmental programs. Monsanto Company, for example, has been an early and active proponent of sustainable production. Monsanto's CEO, Robert B. Shapiro, has set a strong management commitment to seeking environmentally sustainable new products and technologies. Mr. Shapiro recognizes the importance of sustainability to future generations, but also appreciates the opportunities for revenue growth through the development of sustainable production (Magretta, 1997). Monsanto and other chemicals industry companies have been criticized as serious environmental offenders in the past. Because of this criticism, they have been able to see the strategic advantages of sustainable production well before many other companies.

Monsanto has numerous bioengineering initiatives involving the development of plants that can defend themselves against common pests. These initiatives may result in enormous reductions in the need for pesticide application. Likewise, Monsanto is developing chemically designed products that are more environmentally friendly, more easily recycled, and more efficient. In other words, these products are *sustainably designed*.

As early as 1995, Monsanto began to mobilize internal resources to tackle the issues of sustainability. The company found that employees were eager to participate in projects associated with sustainability. The program has resulted in the development of seven teams, dealing with three different aspects of the sustainability equation, as follows:

Develop better decision-making tools

Eco-Efficiency Team	Mapping and measuring the ecological efficiency of processes.
Full-Cost Accounting Team	Developing methodologies that account for the total cost of making and using a product during its life cycle.
Index Team	Measurement tools for tracking business-unit progress toward sustainability.

Look externally at meeting world needs

New Business/New Products Team	Marketplace value of products and services supporting sustainability.

Water Team   Global water needs.

Global Hunger Team   Technologies to alleviate world hunger.

Education and communication

Communication and   Internal training to achieve a common Mon-

Education Team   santo perspective companywide.

Dow Chemical Company likewise is committed to the concepts of product stewardship.[2] Dow has developed an advisory panel of environmental experts and external interested parties to respond to its board of directors on potential product stewardship efforts.

Baxter International, a medical products company, is a global leader in technologies related to the blood and circulatory system. Its environmental, health, and safety (EHS) policy commits Baxter to sustainable development worldwide. The company has been in the forefront of using EMS to manage environmental issues. In 1991, Baxter established state-of-the-art environmental standards and a certification program that is similar to the ISO 14001 EMS standard. The results of the company's efforts have been impressive. Consider the following:

- Since 1989, nonhazardous waste disposal has been cut by 45 percent worldwide (34 million pounds reduction).
- Since 1989, hazardous and other regulated waste disposal has been cut by 48 percent worldwide (1.2 million pounds reduction).
- In 1996, 58 million pounds of materials were recycled worldwide.

Nonetheless, in mid-1997 the company established further EHS goals for the year 2005. Baxter estimates that the annual savings and cost avoidance

---

At Baxter, we've found that corporate environmental programs, as well as those in the health and safety area, produce important financial benefits. Our experience makes a powerful bottom-line argument for EHS-responsible corporate behavior that should appeal even to companies that haven't yet made EHS issues a priority.

Vernon R. Loucks, Jr.
Chairman and CEO, Baxter International

---

associated with meeting these objectives in the year 2005 will reach $125 million. Baxter has already moved toward sustainability through a management commitment that establishes a culture throughout the company. Not only has Baxter demonstrated that progress can be made toward sustainability, but it has made it a financial advantage.

Product stewardship also has seen significant activity in the electronic equipment industry. Americas Materials Recovery Operations (AMRO) is typical of a new trend toward reclamation of decommissioned electronic equipment. AMRO is a medium-sized subsidiary of Digital Equipment Corporation (DEC) that is engaged in salvaging electronic equipment, and it is very good at it. AMRO was one of the first U.S. companies to certify to ISO 14001. The management of AMRO feels strongly that nothing less than excellence in environmental performance is acceptable. AMRO's operations epitomize end-product stewardship. Its profits depend on finding value in equipment that is no longer valued in the marketplace. The more creative ways AMRO can find to reuse, reclaim, or resell components of electronic equipment, the better its financial bottom line—processing 30 million pounds of material per year, AMRO reclaims approximately 90 percent. Interestingly, Baxter is a client of AMRO.

An important offshoot of the reclamation operations has been the tie to DEC's efforts to design for the environment. Input from AMRO, based on its unique experience base in handling old equipment, has provided DEC with creative ideas for ways to design and construct new equipment to facilitate resource recovery.

In a similar initiative, Hewlett-Packard's Hardware Recycling Organization reclaims 70 percent of the material it receives, 99 percent of which is reused or recycled. Likewise, Hewlett-Packard's commitment to the environment

---

The unprecedented number of rapid changes which have recently had impact on businesses worldwide have resulted in a large volume of surplus, idle, and obsolete equipment. Digital has identified and cultivated markets for much of this equipment.

Digital Equipment Company
Americas Materials Recovery Operation

---

focuses on providing products and services that are environmentally sound throughout their life cycles, and includes the following points:

- Designing products with environmental attributes
- Improving manufacturing processes
- Minimizing product packaging
- Enabling product reuse and recycling

Finally, Xerox Corporation operates an Asset Recycle Management Program which uses previously leased Xerox copiers as a source of parts and components for new equipment.

All of these companies share a common vision and understanding. First is a commitment to environmental improvement. Second is a willingness to try creative approaches to any phase of operations. Third is the important realization that financial gain and sustainability are not mutually exclusive. On the contrary, each of these companies has improved its financial performance through sustainability initiatives.

1.3 The EMS Contribution to Sustainability

The Strategic Advisory Group on the Environment (SAGE) was organized by the International Organization for Standardization (ISO) in 1991, partially in anticipation of the Earth Summit. SAGE was tasked with determining whether ISO should develop an international standard for a systematic approach to environmental management that would be similar in concept to the ISO 9000 quality management standard. It is significant that these discussions started in earnest almost 20 years after the United States and other

---

The general purpose of this international standard is to provide assistance to organizations implementing or improving an EMS. It is consistent with the concept of sustainable development and is compatible with diverse cultural, social and organizational frameworks.

ISO 14004:1996, Section 0.1

---

nations first seriously considered the need to manage environmental impacts. It points out very clearly the important reality that environmental management of regulatory compliance does not, de facto, result in sustainability. On the contrary, compliance with environmental regulations is only one part, albeit an important part, of the formula for achieving sustainability.

ICC1. Corporate Priority: To recognize environmental management as among the highest corporate priorities and as a key determinant to sustainable development; to establish policies, programs and practices for conducting operations in an environmentally sound manner.

ICC2. Integrated Management: To integrate these policies, programs and practices fully into each business as an essential element of management in all its functions.

ICC3. Process of Improvement: To continue to improve policies, programs and environmental performance, taking into account technical developments, scientific understanding, consumer needs and community expectations, with legal regulations as starting point; and to apply the same environmental criteria internationally.

Regulatory compliance, especially in the United States, addresses primarily the output side of the sustainability equation. Environmental regulations, relative to sustainability, put controls on air emissions, wastes disposal, and releases to water and land. They attempt to reduce the overall pollutant load on the planet. This has had significant positive impact over the past 20 years; however, compliance is largely achieved only in the United States and other developed countries. Many developing countries have little or no controls on environmental impacts, and much additional effort needs to be targeted toward bringing their environmental impacts under control. Interestingly, only just over 15 percent of the world's population lives in developed countries, despite the fact that those developed countries create the large majority of the environmental impacts related to emissions and waste disposal. Therefore, bringing emerging countries into environmental compliance with reasonable environmental control limits will have marginal impact and fall far short of achieving sustainability. Short of significantly reducing demand for products and services within existing developing countries, something far beyond compliance with regulatory environmental controls is needed. In our technologically driven global society it is foolish to assume that significant reductions in the demand for products and services is likely.

ICC4. Employee Education: To educate, train and motivate employees to conduct their activities in an environmentally responsible manner.

ICC5. Prior Assessment: To assess environmental impacts before starting a new activity or project and before decommissioning a facility or leaving a site.

ICC6. Products and Services: To develop and provide products or services that have no undue environmental impact and are safe in their intended use, that are efficient in their consumption of energy and natural resources, and that can be recycled, reused, or disposed of safely.

ICC7. Customer Advice: To advise, and where relevant educate, customers, distributors, and the public in the safe use, transportation, storage and disposal of products provided; and to apply similar considerations to the provisions of services.

Enter the concept of EMS to provide the environmental management framework to achieve sustainable production in the workplace. If you cannot reduce the demand for goods and services, then provide the goods and services in a manner consistent with sustainability. That is the link between sustainability and EMS. This linkage is well demonstrated by the way in which companies from around the world have voluntarily confirmed a number of charters and codes of conduct that embody sustainability. One very prominent example is the *Business Charter for Sustainable Development* developed by the International Chamber of Commerce (ICC) and endorsed by well over 1000 companies, including over a quarter of the Fortune 500 corporations.

The charter promotes 16 principles for environmental management. These principles are intended to provide a conceptual bridge between sustainability ideals and operational realities.

ICC8. Facilities and Operations: To develop, design and operate facilities and conduct activities taking into consideration the efficient use of energy and materials, the sustainable use of renewable resources, the minimisation of adverse environmental impact and waste generation, and the safe and responsible disposal of residual wastes.

ICC9. Research: To conduct or support research on the environmental impacts of raw materials, products, processes, emissions, and wastes associated with the enterprise and on the means of minimising such adverse impacts.

ICC10. Precautionary Approach: To modify the manufacture, marketing, or use of products or services or the conduct of activities, consistent with scientific and technical understanding, to prevent serious or irreversible environmental degradation.

Sustainability requires that a company have a corporate awareness of the principles of sustainability for all aspects of its operations. This awareness should be the basis for the company's approach to problem solving and should encourage creative ideas for new technologies, better operational processes, new products or services, and so forth. All stages of a product's life cycle should be considered. An effective environmental strategy for achieving sustainability requires more than the implementation of scattered projects related to pollution prevention or waste minimization. It requires a systematic approach to the way the business is run.

An EMS provides the perfect platform for the type of systematic approach needed to achieve sustainability. The awareness and cultural change that are part and parcel of an effectively implemented EMS provide the appropriate atmosphere for creative ideas to prosper. Likewise, the EMS provides a management system whose elements can point the company toward the path of

ICC11. Contractors and Suppliers: To promote the adoption of these principles by contractors acting on behalf of the enterprise, encouraging and, where appropriate, requiring improvements in their practices to make them consistent with those of the enterprise; and to encourage the wider adoption of these principles by suppliers.

ICC12. Emergency Preparedness: To develop and maintain, where significant hazards exist, emergency preparedness plans in conjunction with the emergency services, relevant authorities and the local community, recognizing potential transboundary impacts.

ICC13. Transfer of Technology: To contribute to the transfer of environmentally sound technology and management methods throughout the industrial and public sectors.

ICC14. Contributing to the Common Effect: To contribute to the development of public policy and to business, governmental and intergovernmental programs and educational initiatives that will enhance environmental awareness and protection.

ICC15. Openness to Concerns: To foster openness and dialogue with employees and the public, anticipating and responding to their concerns about potential hazards and impacts of operations, products, wastes or services, including those of transboundary or global significance.

ICC16. Compliance and Reporting: To measure environmental performance; to conduct regular environmental audits and assessments of compliance with company requirements, legal requirements and these principles; and periodically to provide appropriate information to the Board of Directors, shareholders, employees, the authorities and the public.

sustainable production, can provide the tools to ensure that its operations are consistent with sustainable production, and can provide the data to demonstrate the effectiveness of its efforts.

As seen from the companies discussed in this chapter and as will become evident as you read further in this book, those who have been progressive in their approach to environmental management have had systems in place to provide continuity, to define roles and assign responsibilities, to encourage creative problem solving, and to measure their success. Whether they call it an EMS or follow any specific EMS guidance, these progressive companies have more than just random programs in place. They all have a strong management commitment and a coordinated approach to achieving their goals. The emphasis on EMS is a recognition that to achieve sustainability, a systematic approach is essential.

CHAPTER 2

TRENDS AND DRIVERS FOR ENVIRONMENTAL MANAGEMENT

Regulation sets mixed goals, drains resources and does not encourage risk taking. Regulation is a miserable and inefficient substitute for leadership. American companies must lead, must supply the vision necessary for a pollution free future. The workplace should be the laboratory and the classroom for this cultural shift.

DENNY J. BEROIZ—1992
DIRECTOR, ENVIRONMENTAL RESOURCE MANAGEMENT
NORTHROP B-2 DIVISION

2.1   Changes Are Warranted

From its modest beginnings in 1970, the U.S. Environmental Protection Agency (EPA) by 1990 had grown to a staff of nearly 18,000 and had an operating budget of $4.5 billion, or about a seventh of the staff and a third of the spending of the entire federal regulatory machine. From 1986 to 1991, the number of pages of environmental regulations published in the Code of the Federal Register more than doubled, from under 9,000 to over 18,000. In 1992, by EPA's own estimates, complying with its regulations was costing the country some $115 billion per year—equal to 2.1 percent of the Gross National Product (GNP)—and some economists believed this number to be a serious underestimate of the actual impact on the GNP. Not all of the blame could be placed on EPA's shoulders, however. As can be seen in Table 2.1, congressional environmental activism greatly increased starting in the 1960s, resulting in an explosion of regulatory directives. This congressional zeal resulted in a patchwork of media-specific programs that in many instances tied the environmental agency's hands.

TABLE 2.1. The Growth of U.S. Environmental Legislation

Year	Federal legislation
1899	Refuse Act
1940	Bald and Golden Eagle Protection Act
1947	Insecticide, Fungicide and Rodenticide Act
1948	Water Pollution Control Act
1956	Fish and Wildlife Act
1963	Clean Air Act
1964	Wilderness Act
1965	Water Quality Act, Solid Waste Disposal Act, Anadromous Fish Conservation Act
1966	NEPA established, Clean Water Restoration Act
1967	Air Quality Act
1968	Wild and Scenic Rivers Act
1969	National Environmental Quality Act
1970	USEPA created, Clean Air Amendment Act
1972	Coastal Zone Management Act, Clean Water Act, Marine Mammal Protection Act
1973	Endangered Species Act
1974	Safe Drinking Water Act
1976	Toxic Substances Control Act, Resource Conservation and Recovery Act
1977	Clean Water Act Amendments, Clean Air Act Amendments
1980	Comprehensive Environmental Response, Compensation, and Liability Act (Superfund)
1986	Right-to-Know Act
1987	Water Quality Act
1990	Pollution Prevention Act, Clean Air Act Amendments

Most corporations are deservedly proud of the progress they have made in reducing their impact on the environment over the preceding several decades, and admit that much of this progress was the direct result of their necessary response to increasingly stricter environmental laws and regulations imposed at the national, state, and sometimes regional levels. Undoubtedly the command-and-control approach to environmental improvement was necessary to jumpstart wholesale restoration and protection measures in the United States. But the response of business and industry to the upward spiral of accelerating regulatory burdens was also understandable and was largely characterized by the following:

- Focusing on compliance with specific permit conditions and meeting the letter of the law; no volunteering for any "extras"
- Little desire or incentive for external communications on environmental matters
- Adversarial relationships with regulators and environmental interest groups and extensive use of legal counsel
- A fragmented media-by-media approach to addressing environmental requirements
- An environmental or environmental, health, and safety (EHS) function viewed as a separate entity, often as purely a cost center/ overhead function with no connection to the organization's core processes or services (essentially relegating EHS to an adjunct operation—"Don't call us, we'll call you!")
- Limited involvement by executive management or board of directors with company environmental matters

The nature of the inflexible regulatory command-and-control system and the cascading effect of federal, state, and local regulations resulted in U.S. industry adopting a largely reactionary approach to environmental responsibilities (a "necessary evil," as one veteran manager described it). Government at multiple levels set the framework for compliance and industry responded— or faced the consequences of notices of violation, fines, penalties, civil or criminal court proceedings, and judgment in the court of public opinion. Larger companies staffed to whatever levels were necessary to meet the organization's compliance requirements, which was a resource-intensive effort with virtually 100 percent of those highly capable resources (environmental managers and staff) being dedicated to compliance as virtually their sole target.

Smaller companies struggled to keep abreast of the rapidly unfolding regulatory requirements and faced financial burdens to maintain the EHS staff necessary to reach and maintain compliance. For many of these smaller companies overwhelmed by regulatory requirements, simply flying below the radar became a common tactic—keeping a low profile and hoping that regulatory agency inspectors had their hands full with larger concerns. As one former environmental manager expressed, "In those early days, full compliance was just a dream, an unattainable goal for many companies. Management thought that being in compliance 'most of the time' was good enough." Even the most conscientious of companies often felt that they were always one run behind and just as they thought they might tie the score to catch up, the rules changed!

When individual companies did seek to accept their environmental responsibilities willingly and worked diligently to attain full compliance, they often still faced unsympathetic regulators and a public that had already formed its negative opinion of industry. Corporate leaders themselves were reluctant to raise their organizations' environmental profiles in the least, choosing most often to avoid public discussion of environmental matters if at all possible. This low-profile strategy was the norm even when a firm had success stories to relate in the areas of pollution control, waste minimization, and toxicity reductions. As in Army life, "Don't volunteer" was the pre-1990 credo for most corporate environmental managers and the executives to whom they reported. With compliance as the driving and singular goal, the system awarded no company bonus points for going beyond that compliance line.

By 1990, many leaders in industry were vocal in questioning the wisdom of continuing this upward legislative and regulatory spiral. While a few federal and state leaders were sympathetic to industry's concerns, the environmental performance bar—unlike a goal line—did not remain stationary, even with the passage of the last link in a long chain of major federal environmental laws, the Clear Air Act Amendments of 1990. The bar continued to rise because the drivers for environmental improvements were changing and evolving: Compliance was no longer the satisfactory end point. It was becoming clear to regulators and the regulated alike that command-and-control approaches, while far from dead, were not going to remain the preferred vehicle for advancing meaningful environmental protection and improvement efforts in the future.

2.2 Trends and New Drivers for Environmental Improvements

Over the years, the extent of our national commitment to environmental improvement has been clarified, and surrogate regulators and voluntary drivers have emerged.

2.2.1 Clarification of Our Public Environmental Ethic

In the early 1980s, one of the hallmarks of the Reagan administration was regulatory relief for U.S. businesses, and, ultimately, the consumers they served. In most areas of regulatory matters, this policy was well received and supported by a public that realized that overregulation was a severe hindrance in a free economy. But the public judged deregulation initiatives quite selectively and on their own merits. When the administration appointed its choice for EPA administrator, Anne Gorsuch (1981 to 1983), she was quickly judged to be too probusiness and too prone to weaken the environmental protection measures won during the previous decade. Under fire for Gorsuch's poor relationship with Congress and the sharp reductions in EPA's budget and personnel levels, the Reagan administration learned a hard lesson: Broad support for environmental protection did not rest solely with environmental activist groups but was embraced by the public. These public and congressional concerns led President Reagan to make dramatic changes. Gorsuch's short tenure was ended by a return of the agency's first administrator, William Ruckelshaus, an individual widely respected in both environmental and business circles.

Strong public support for environmental measures has only increased over the years. Periodically, the *Wall Street Journal* and NBC have conducted a poll on environmental issues asking for a response to the following statement:

> *Protecting the environment is so important that requirements and standards cannot be too high and continuing environmental improvements must be made regardless of cost.*

In 1981, 45 percent of the respondents said they agreed with that statement and 42 percent disagreed. When the poll question was repeated in 1991, 90 percent of the respondents claimed they agreed with the same statement. The evidence of this broad public support for strong environmental protection was confirmed by the backlash Congress experienced in the 1994 elections after it sought to weaken such measures under the umbrella of regulatory reform. The public was sympathetic to reform, but not to what it perceived as a wholesale threat to the protective measures won through the previous decades of legislative activity. Thus, the environmental performance bar for industry has been set not only by direct legislative or regulatory actions, but by the increasing expectations of the public that is employed by, served by, or affected by that industry. And those constituencies clearly want the performance bar to continue to rise.

William Reilly served as the EPA administrator from 1989 to 1993, a pivotal period for changing the fundamental approaches the country would take toward environmental protection. In an April 30, 1992, speech to the National Press Club on the new environmentalism, Administrator Reilly stated:

> *The environment-versus-economy formulation that has characterized so much of the environmental policy debate in America for the past 20 years is increasingly rejected by both the public and leading elements of the business community. In the newly emerging marketplace, the green of environmental protection is beginning to form a ready alliance with the green of profits. A new environmentalism is taking shape in this country; it integrates environment and economics.*

Later that same year, Reilly reinforced these thoughts when he told a gathering of Republican governors:

> *I believe that the climate is right to encourage corporate America to do better than what the laws require, to ask them more basic questions, and then to reward them for that kind of performance.*

In seeking to integrate environmental goals with the nation's economic goals, Reilly initiated several specific outreach efforts to industry to encourage the movement toward voluntary environmental protection efforts, efforts that would achieve results beyond what regulations were accomplishing, or perhaps could accomplish. Under his leadership the agency launched the Green Lights program, designed to encourage companies to perform energy audits and install energy-efficient lighting.

A second early initiative of Reilly's administration was the highly successful 33/50 program, which stressed a voluntary, collaborative, and flexible approach to pollution prevention. In 1988, there were 1.4 billion pounds of releases or transfers of 17 priority pollutants reported to the EPA Toxic Release Inventory (TRI; see following list). The 33/50 program aimed to cut this figure in half by 1995—a 700 million pound reduction—with an interim goal of a 33-percent reduction by 1992, by challenging industry to voluntarily reduce its emissions to the environment by these amounts, or more. Ultimately, over 1100 firms responded to this call for voluntary participation, including such well-known names as General Motors, W.R. Grace, the Gillette Company, and 3M, whose award-winning program, Pollution Prevention Pays (3P), had been up and running since 1975. By 1994, the 33/50 initiative could claim success as releases of TRI chemicals had declined by 50 percent from the 1988 base year, a year ahead of the 1995 target.

The 17 Target Chemicals on the EPA Toxic Release Inventory

Benzene	Methyl isobutyl ketone
Cadmium and compounds	Methylene chloride
Carbon tetrachloride	Nickel and compounds
Chloroform	Tetrachloroethylene
Chromium and compounds	Toluene
Cyanides	Trichloroethane
Lead and compounds	Trichloroethylene
Mercury and compounds	Xylenes
Methyl ethyl ketone	

The Global Environmental Management Initiative (GEMI) commissioned a survey in the mid 1000s to examine industry's voluntarily driven incentives for engaging in environmental improvements (Yoshi and Herbst, 1996). Overseen by GEMI's work group on Incentives, Disincentives, Environmental Performance, and Accountability for the 21st Century (IDEA 21), the researchers interviewed executives from 19 companies that had participated in the EPA 33/50 program. When asked about the factors that motivated their companies to participate in this voluntary program, the reasons provided included the following:

- The initiative dovetailed with internal efforts to reduce environmental releases.
- The project was goal or results oriented, with flexibility provided to set company-specific goals.
- There were public relations benefits from participating, given the high level of visibility of public and media attention on TRI releases.
- The participation criteria were simple.

- The initiative provided an opportunity to improve regulatory relations.
- 33/50 was the first initiative of this kind, and its novelty stimulated private sector interest.
- EPA management aggressively sought company participation.
- There was minimal risk, legal or otherwise, from participating.
- Signing up for 33/50 helped to meet expectations created from enrollment in other industry initiatives, such as Responsible Care®.

One leadership company that rallied early to the 33/50 call was HADCO Corporation of Salem, New Hampshire. HADCO is a global developer and supplier of high-quality electronic interconnect products and services with approximately $650 million in annual sales. In 1991, HADCO received a letter from EPA Administrator Reilly challenging it to join the 33/50 program, and it joined that year, along with 236 other firms, including 7 from its home state.

HADCO's incentives to participate in Reilly's initiative were straightforward: As one of the top 600 TRI emitters in the nation and the number-1 emitter in New Hampshire, it had received its share of bad publicity. Claims Lee Wilmot, HADCO's Director of Safety, Health, and Environmental Affairs, "Since the summer of 1989 when the first TRI results were publicly reported, we had received two years of 'black eyes.' Headquartered in a state that cares greatly for its natural resources and quality of life, we needed to show good faith." HADCO set a stretch goal for itself by any measure: a remarkable 98-percent reduction in emissions of TRI chemicals by 1995. This high-tech manufacturer rolled up its corporate sleeves and exceeded even its stretch goal with a 99.5-percent reduction, dropping out of the state's top ten TRI emitters even as other industries were following suit and rapidly reducing their emissions.

Another advanced technology company that credits the TRI reporting requirements with triggering an internal cultural change is Lockheed Sanders, part of the Lockheed-Martin family. TRI reporting meant that Lockheed Sanders had to measure its chemical losses for the first time, and that awareness led its engineers and environmental staff to examine processes that previously had gone unquestioned. In one particular process, nearly 90 percent of the organic TRI compound used was found to be lost to the atmosphere. Further assessment determined that the process itself was actually nonessential to the product line, and the process was shut down within three days, saving both materials and cost. Lockheed Sanders met its 33/50 goals because it found meet-ing them to be the *right* thing to do, both economically and environmentally.

Even as fundamental improvements were occurring in the realm of envi-ronmental management, progressive corporate leaders realized that the envi-ronmental performance and expectation bar was constantly rising. Leading companies were publicly stating their understanding that environmental pro-tection was moving past the strict goal of compliance into the realm of stew-ardship issues, as indicated by this 1989 Anheuser-Busch Companies print advertisement:

> *As our nation moves into the 21st century, American industry will be called upon to meet ever higher standards of environmental stewardship. All com-panies must accept the challenge—being mindful not only of their regulatory obligations and controls, but also of promoting environmental awareness in everything they do.*
>
> *At Anheuser-Busch, we not only accept this responsibility—we welcome it. Just as we apply exacting standards to brewing of our quality beers so must we adopt an uncompromising stance when it comes to protecting the environment. And we urge other members of the business community to do the same.*
>
> *After all, quality companies have a sense of commitment—to their cus-tomers, their employees, the communities where they do business . . . and to the environment. People deserve a quality environment now, and in the future.*

Other early-1990-era indications that organizations were understanding the potential impacts of the public's concern for environmental responsibility could be found in professional surveys of corporate leaders. In 1992, the pro-fessional firm of Fredrikson & Byron conducted telephone interviews with executives of 110 of the largest manufacturing firms in Minnesota. Among the survey's findings were the following:

- 65 percent of the responding executives cited the possibility of dam-age to their company's public image as the major factor contributing to their approach to compliance.
- Executives tended to be as concerned about image and employee dissatisfaction as they were about revocation of permits or licenses and other punitive measures.

- 53 percent believed that being proactive in addressing environmental issues would give them a competitive advantage by enhancing their public image and by positioning them to offer products environmentally acceptable to their clients.

In the fall of 1992, Coopers & Lybrand surveyed the CEOs and senior management of more than 100 New England businesses on behalf of the New England Council, a prominent regional business organization. When these corporate executives were asked to list the factors that motivated their companies' environmental activities, the categories of social responsibility and corporate image together accounted for 34 percent, which was equal to the combined categories of compliance with regulations and preventing incidents.

The times were indeed changing, and the balance between regulatory-driven and voluntary environmental activities was shifting, as Figure 2.1 diagrammatically reflects.

2.2.2 The Role of Surrogate Regulators

Many of the new drivers for environmental improvement are nonregulatory, at least in the sense that they are not related to direct requirements imposed by environmental agencies. In a real sense, however, these drivers function as

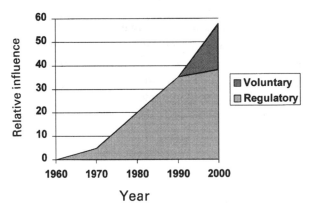

FIGURE 2.1. The shifting balance of regulatory–voluntary drivers on U.S. industry.

surrogate regulators and thus many of them may still be considered more "stick" than "carrot." Three of the new surrogate environmental regulators with which U.S. corporations increasingly must contend follow:

- *Securities and Exchange Commission (SEC) and GAAP Disclosure Requirements.* Environmental liability disclosure requirements for publicly traded companies following generally accepted accounting principles (GAAP).
- *Department of Justice Sentencing Guidelines.* "Factors in Decisions on Criminal Prosecutions for Environmental Violations in the Context of Significant Voluntary Compliance or Disclosure Efforts by the Violator": It is the policy of the Department of Justice to encourage self-auditing, self-policing, and voluntary disclosure of environmental violations by the regulated community by indicating that these activities are viewed as mitigating factors in the Department's exercise of criminal environmental enforcement discretion (U.S. Department of Justice, July 1991).
- *EPA Final Audit Policy.* Developed in close consultation with the Department of Justice and published in December 1995, "Incentives for Self-Policing: Discovery, Disclosure, Correction and Prevention of Violations" outlines the agency's policy statement concerning the conditions under which it will reduce the gravity component of civil penalties and not seek criminal prosecution for environmental violations.

Other surrogate regulators, several of which are discussed in Chapters 10 and 11, are the following:

- Corporate officer and board of director liability
- Lending institution requirements
- Investor concerns and expectations
- Customer requirements and expectations
- International trade
- Community right-to-know initiatives

No doubt additional surrogate regulators will evolve in time—insurance companies, for example, seeking to tie coverage for a company's accidental environmental damage to such requirements as stringent operating controls, an internal environmental oversight committee, or the establishment of a formal and verifiable EMS.

2.2.3 The Voluntary Drivers

While we have described 1990 as a year when our regulation-driven approach to environmental improvements began to be seriously challenged, 1995 was an equally pivotal period. The change of party leadership in the U.S. Congress (the so-called Republican Revolution resulting from the 1994 fall elections) led to a virtual explosion of deregulation initiatives and budget battles. All federal agencies (and state agencies that depended upon federal grants) began to address their own performance and accomplishments in light of the "What are we getting for our budget dollars?" questions and the reinvention of government initiatives.

As a result of EPA's position in the congressional spotlight, the agency looked hard at the issues of measuring real environmental performance and driving progress improvements by more than regulatory measures. EPA moved itself toward greater efficiency in conducting its agency mission and it offered a new round of voluntary programs to industry, such as Environmental Leadership; XL; the Common Sense Initiative; and EPA New England's Star-Track program, with a third-party certification component. Some of these initiatives have proven to be more workable or acceptable than others, but the trend is clear: performance-based incentives to environmental compliance and beyond-compliance improvements—more carrots.

Some other categories of largely or wholly voluntary drivers that provide incentives for many industry sectors or individual companies include the following:

- Corporate reputation concerns
- Sustainable development concerns
- Industry-specific codes of practice
- Product stewardship and life-cycle management practices
- Pollution prevention initiatives
- Integration of management systems (including ISO 9000)
- Business performance improvement and economic value added efforts

- Management of risks
- Regulatory relief opportunities

Several of these drivers will be discussed in detail in the subsequent chapters on EMS and management system integration efforts.

2.3 Responding to Drivers—Opportunities for Improvement

Progressive companies have sought avenues to best respond to the myriad new drivers influencing their operations and governance activities. Sustainable development, stewardship of resources, and environmental ethics relate to, and help define, an organization's culture and its response to current and future drivers.

2.3.1 Sustainable Development and Stewardship

As discussed in Chapter 1, the concept of sustainable development is based on the observation that many of the natural resources society uses either are finite or are renewable only if properly utilized and managed. Creating a balance between the utilization of resources for current societal needs and the capacity of natural systems to provide those resources yields sustainable development.

Globally, it was a U.N. initiative that brought focus to the concept of sustainability and sustainable development issues. Attended by representatives of over 170 countries, the Earth Summit reviewed the environmental progress that had occurred since earlier UN conferences held in 1972 and 1982. Among the outcomes of this 1992 conference was the Rio Declaration on Environment and Development, with 27 principles for sustainable development (referred to as Agenda 21). As an example, Principle 4 states:

> In order to achieve sustainable development, environmental protection shall constitute an integral part of the development process and cannot be considered in isolation from it.

In the United States, the issue of sustainable development was brought to the forefront with the June 1993 creation of the President's Council on Sustainable Development, formed as a direct result of the U.N. Earth Summit. The council is a groundbreaking partnership of diverse leaders from business, government, and nongovernmental organizations (NGOs). Among the 30-plus council members, industry has been represented by many prominent business leaders, including the following:

> David T. Buzelli, Vice President and Corporate Director, The Dow Chemical Company (who served as the Council's first cochair with Jonathan Lash, President, World Resources Institute)
> Richard Barth, Chairman, President and CEO, Ciba-Geigy Corporation
> Richard A. Clarke, Chairman and CEO, Pacific Gas and Electric Company (retired)
> A. D. "Pete" Correll, Chairman and CEO, Georgia-Pacific Corporation
> Kenneth T. Derr, Chairman and CEO, Chevron Corporation
> William E. Hoglund, Executive Vice President, General Motors Corporation (retired)
> Samuel C. Johnson, Chairman, S.C. Johnson & Son., Inc.
> Kenneth L. Lay, Chairman and CEO, Enron Corporation
> William D. Ruckelshaus, Chairman, Browning-Ferris Industries, Inc. (and former two-term EPA Administrator)

The council's early efforts culminated in a February 1996 report titled *Sustainable America: A New Consensus for Prosperity, Opportunity, and a Healthy Environment for the Future.* In examining the U.S. system of environmental management that had been built largely since 1970, the Council acknowledged that the singular command-and-control regulatory approach needed to yield to a wider range of strategic environmental protection approaches to achieve the objectives of sustainable development. It concluded that the lessons of the past 25 years could be summarized as follows:

- Economic, environmental, and social problems cannot be addressed in isolation. Economic prosperity, environmental quality, and social equity need to be pursued simultaneously.
- Science-based national standards that protect human health and the environment are the foundation of any effective system of environmental protection.

- The adversarial nature of the current system precludes solutions that become possible when potential adversaries cooperate and collaborate.
- Technology-based regulation can sometimes encourage technological innovation, but it can also stifle it; pollution prevention is better than pollution control.
- Enhanced flexibility for achieving environmental goals, coupled with strong compliance assurance mechanisms—including enforcement—can spur private sector innovation that will enhance environmental protection at a substantially lower cost both to individual firms and to society as a whole.
- Science, economics, and societal values should be considered in making decisions. Quality information is essential to sound decision making.
- Many state governments have developed significant environmental management capacity. Indeed, many of the most creative and lasting solutions arise from collaborations involving federal, state, local, and tribal governments in places where problems exist—from urban communities to watersheds.

From these summary conclusions, the council went on to closely evaluate the development of a more cost-effective environmental management system based on performance, flexibility, and accountability. Based upon underlying principles of greater regulatory flexibility and partnerships, the council made the following recommendations:

> The Nation should pursue two paths in reforming environmental regulation. The first is to improve the efficiency and effectiveness of the current environmental management system. The second is to develop and test innovative approaches and create a new alternative environmental management system that achieves more protection at a lower cost.

Seven policy recommendations were then put forth by the council in its report:

1. *Increase cost-effectiveness of the existing regulatory system.* Accelerate efforts to evaluate existing regulations and to create opportunities for attaining environmental goals at lower economic costs.

2. *Create an alternative performance-based management system.* Create a bold new alternative environmental management system designed to achieve superior environmental protection and economic development that relies on verifiable and enforceable performance-based standards and provides increased operational flexibility through a collaborative decision-making process.

3. *Adopt extended product stewardship.* Adopt a voluntary system that ensures responsibility for the environmental effects throughout a product's life cycle by all those involved in the life cycle. The greatest opportunity for extended product responsibility rests with those throughout the commerce chain—designers, suppliers, manufacturers, distributors, users, and disposers—that are in a position to practice resource conservation and pollution prevention at lower cost.

4. *Shift tax policies.* Begin the long-term process of shifting to tax policies that—without increasing overall tax burdens—encourage employment and economic opportunity while discouraging environmentally damaging production and consumption decisions.

5. *Reform subsidy policy.* Eliminate government subsidies that encourage activities inconsistent with economic, environmental, and social goals.

6. *Use market incentives.* Make greater use of market incentives as part of an overall environmental management system to achieve environmental and natural resource management objectives whenever feasible. This system must provide for verification, accountability, and the means to ensure that national standards are met or exceeded.

7. *Create intergovernmental partnerships.* Create intergovernmental partnerships to pursue economic prosperity, environmental protection, and social equity in an integrated way.

Obviously, many of these suggestions go well into the realm of national policymaking and are beyond the control of any individual company or even any single industrial sector. At first, creating this balance within a business framework does seem daunting. How can one company predict the future needs of society and respond appropriately? What is a corporation's responsibility in advancing the principles of global sustainability? The basis for answering these questions lies in the arena of business strategy and its linkage to a company's culture and environmental ethics.

The term *environmental ethic* implies that a corporation is interested not only in meeting the bare requirements of regulatory compliance, but in moving to a position of continuous improvement toward sustainability. It requires a recognition that complying with environmental regulations is just one hurdle in the race to stay competitive and produce value for shareholders. Corporations with an interest in sustainability recognize environmental impacts as a cost, both to their direct operations and to society at large.

The President's Council on Sustainable Development put it this way:

> *Without personal and collective commitment, without an ethic based on the acceptance of responsibility, efforts to sustain natural resources protection and environmental quality cannot succeed.*

Progressive corporations have adopted many practices in recent years to limit their impact on the environment, including recycling, waste minimization, and prevention of pollution at its source. While these programs may be good in and of themselves, many were developed in an ad hoc manner without the benefit of an integrated business strategy and without clear commitment from executive management. The concepts of sustainability and stewardship imply a profound change in the way corporations manage themselves. Many leading companies are moving forcefully toward integrated management approaches that address environmental issues and business issues as one and the same.

2.3.2 Management Principles and Codes

Management principles are guidelines or codes of practice adopted voluntarily by organizations. These principles may originate with an industry trade association, an independent oversight organization, or the individual company itself. They are not a management system, per se, but they very much need the framework of a management system to be implemented in any effective fashion.

Examples of company-developed management principles include corporate mission statements and environmental policy statements. Such statements express in writing that organization's beliefs, values, and principles and serve as critical guidelines for its corporate actions, activities, and goals. *Guiding principles* is an appropriate term used within several organizations. Chapter 3 explores in some detail the issues of corporate mission statements and environmental policy statements and provides some examples of their current use.

An industry-specific code of management principles that most environmental professionals are at least familiar with is the Chemical Manufacturers Association (CMA) Responsible Care initiative. Developed in the 1980s for member companies of this national trade association, adherence to Responsible Care environmental, health, and safety principles is now a requirement for CMA membership. The code promotes the following ten Guiding Principles, which are the foundation for the Responsible Care ethic:

1. To recognize and respond to community concerns about chemicals and our operations.
2. To develop and produce chemicals that can be manufactured, transported, used, and disposed of safely.
3. To make health, safety, and environmental considerations a priority in our planning for all existing and new products and processes.
4. To report promptly to officials, employees, customers, and the public, information on chemical-related health or environmental hazards and to recommend protective measures.
5. To counsel customers on the safe use, transportation, and disposal of chemical products.
6. To operate our plants and facilities in a manner that protects the environment and the health and safety of our employees and the public.
7. To extend knowledge by conducting or supporting research on the health, safety, and environmental effects of our products, processes, and waste materials.
8. To work with others to resolve problems created by past handling and disposal of hazardous substances.
9. To participate with government and others in creating responsible laws, regulations, and standards to safeguard the community, workplace, and environment.
10. To promote the principles and practices of Responsible Care by sharing experiences and offering assistance to others who produce, handle, use, transport, or dispose of chemicals.

These ten Guiding Principles are then supported by six Codes of Management Practice, which specifically address the following concerns:

1. Pollution prevention
2. Worker health and safety
3. Process safety
4. Distribution
5. Product stewardship
6. Community awareness and emergency response

Taken together, the CMA Guiding Principles and Codes of Management Practice permit member companies to align their management systems and programs for conformance. CMA membership is held by approximately 190 companies, including most major and many smaller chemical firms in the United States. Larger members include Monsanto Company, BASF Corporation, DuPont, Dow Chemical Company, 3M, Bayer Corporation, and Merck & Company, Inc. Other firms that hold CMA membership include: Praxair, Inc., Quantum Chemical Company, Henkel Corporation, and ICI Americas, Inc.

CMA's Responsible Care initiative has been assessed by many other industry trade associations, and adaptations of CMA's approach have been adopted for use by their members. Noteworthy examples from U.S.-based trade organizations include the following:

- American Forest and Paper Association (Sustainable Forestry Initiative)
- American Petroleum Institute (Strategies for Today's Environmental Partnership [STEP] initiative)
- National Association of Chemical Distributors (Responsible Distribution Process)
- National Paint and Coatings Association (Coatings Care™)

As an example of this successful adaptation of the Responsible Care approach, the National Paint and Coatings Association reported that by 1997 nearly half of its 400 members, representing manufacturing and raw materials suppliers and distributors, were participating in the Coatings Care program and its Codes of Management Practices.

Similarly, the American Petroleum Institute (API) has developed 7 key strategies to guide the petroleum industry's operations and 11 specific environmental principles that are embodied in the organization's by-laws. The STEP program represents the industry's collective initiatives to improve EHS performance, document and communicate achievements, and improve the public's understanding of the performance issues.

Other countries have built upon CMA's example. In the United Kingdom, the Chemical Industries Association (CIA) publishes guidance on implementing Responsible Care principles, and the European Chemical Industry Council (CEFIC) headquartered in Brussels developed a harmonized set of core Responsible Care performance indicators. The Chemical and Allied Industries Association (CAIA) of South Africa launched that country's responsible care initiative in 1994.

An example of a nonprofit, nonpartisan organization with voluntary membership is the Coalition for Environmentally Responsible Economies (CERES), based in Boston. CERES members agree to abide by a uniform set of principles and report their environmental progress annually. These reports are unranked but are made publicly available. Additional discussion on the CERES approach to voluntary environmental performance reporting is found in Chapter 9.

One of the most significant sets of environmental management principles that is truly international in application and universally applicable to any industry or industrial sector is the Business Charter for Sustainable Development created by the International Chamber of Commerce (ICC), headquartered in Paris. The Business Charter was prepared for and presented at the Second World Industry Conference on Environmental Management in 1991 to guide actions by corporations and business organizations. The GEMI organization of Washington, D.C., has developed a system patterned after the ICC's 16 principles to assist companies in implementing the ICC Charter—the GEMI Environmental Self-Assessment Program (Figure 2.2).

Adoption of the ICC Charter or CMA's Responsible Care initiative does not in and of itself establish a well-functioning, robust environmental management system. Rather it is a statement of principles of what the organization intends to achieve and what will serve as its guideposts as it implements a management system to accomplish those objectives.

Compliance & reporting

Openness to concerns

Common efforts

Technology transfer

Emergency prepared- ness

Contractors & suppliers

Precautionary approach

Research

ICC

Corporate priority

Integrated management

Process of improvement

Employee education

Prior assessment

Products & services

Customer advice

Facilities & operations

FIGURE 2.2. The elements of the ICC charter.

2.3.3 Environmental Management Systems

Environmental management systems (EMS) are a major topic of discussion among environmental professionals, especially since the publication of the ISO 14001 EMS standards in September 1996. Many EMS practitioners are also familiar with the precursor to ISO 14001, the British Standard BS-7750, and with the European Union's system standards, the Eco-Management and Auditing Scheme (EMAS).

Generically, an EMS is simply a process to assist a company in addressing its environmental impacts and setting goals and targets for meeting its defined environmental responsibilities. As with any management system, an EMS is a structured approach that defines key organizational elements, roles, responsibilities, policies, procedures, processes, and required resources. To be effective, an EMS needs to be comprehensive, quality-driven, and integrated with other management systems. Leading organizations have come to realize that an effective environmental management process:

- Is a critical strategic business issue
- Is an enterprisewide core process
- Affects every point in the value chain

- Affects business risk
- Affects customer and stakeholder satisfaction
- Affects product and process quality
- Affects shareholder value

The challenges in implementing a fully functioning EMS within a business organization are many. Historically, most firms have addressed environmental concerns on an ad hoc, often media-specific, basis. The efforts were not specifically driven by focused corporate goals or processes and understandably lacked integration and continuity. The basic transition from a *reactive* process to a *proactive* one is not without difficulty.

In 1996, KPMG's Canadian Environmental Risk Management Practice surveyed over 400 companies with respect to their EMS issues (KPMG, 1996). While approximately 64 percent reported that they possessed an effective EMS, only 15 percent of those firms in fact conformed to all of the EMS elements presented in the questionnaire. This conformance number has increased dramatically from a similar KPMG survey conducted in 1994, which found only 2.5 percent in full conformance (with a less rigorous set of EMS elements). The 1996 survey, however, found that *firefighting* was still a popular approach to environmental management, with 57 percent of those organizations that lacked an EMS reporting dealing with issues on only an *as required* basis. Additional discussion from this KPMG survey concerning performance measures is presented in Section 2.3.4 and in Chapter 9.

Many management system *elements* should be generic to virtually any complete EMS, even if the system was developed internally by a company's staff to suit its particular needs and culture (i.e., "home grown"). In practice, different companies will combine some management elements and perhaps not include others, or some elements (risk management or budgeting and accounting, for instance) will not be considered strictly part of the EMS. In our experience, 14 to 18 distinct system elements are common to most robust EMSs and can be identified and assessed by internal or external reviewers. Common elements include the following:

- Organization and structure
- Management support
- Organizational culture

- Quality and quantity of human and physical resources
- Policies and procedures
- Training and awareness
- Communication, both internal and external
- Planning
- Continuous improvement and performance measurement
- Regulatory tracking and regulatory relationships
- Auditing and assurance
- Environmental (or EHS) management information systems
- Risk management
- Budgeting and accounting
- Records and documentation

Section II of this book discusses the design and implementation of formal Environmental Management Systems, especially in the context of the growing popularity of the ISO 14001 approach, and discusses the options for certification of your EMS. Section III discusses some of these management system elements (such as environmental accounting) in the framework of integrating quality, environmental and business management systems.

2.3.4 Increased Responsibility for Corporate Officers and Directors

A strong driver for companies to improve their environmental performance is the increasing corporate and personal liability of officers members of the board of directors for the firm's environmental violations. Not surprisingly, senior managers are recognizing and responding to this liability driver. The 1996 KPMG survey of Canadian companies discussed earlier in this chapter indicated that responsibility for environmental management was assigned at the senior management level in 69 percent of the firms surveyed (Table 2.2). The senior management role increased to 85 percent among those firms with a formal EMS in place. These results indicate that environmental issues are being addressed primarily at the policy level—strong evidence of senior manager commitment and consistent with survey results showing that board of director liability concerns rank among the top three motivating factors that influence organizations to take action on environmental issues:

TABLE 2.2. 1996 KPMG Survey of Canadian Companies— Percentage of Respondents with Critical Elements in their Environmental Management Systems

Critical element	Percent
Process to identify and analyze legal requirement	69
Objectives and targets consistent with the environmental policy	50
Time frames for targets	44
Responsibility for environmental management assigned at:	
Senior management level	69
Middle management level	48
Staff level	32
Operating procedures for environmental performance	65
Environmental procurement policies and procedures	38
Appropriate training for personnel	71
Risk assessment process for environmental risks	50
Communication strategy for environmental management and performance	48
Internal communications system	53
External communication of environmental performance	42
Periodic review or audit of EMS	56
Continuous improvement of EMS	56

- Compliance with regulations
- Board of director liability
- Employees

The primary responsibilities of the board of directors are to ensure that the organization appropriately manages and minimizes the risks that environmental matters pose to business and to set the corporate ethical culture. The board deals with strategic issues related to marketing, trade, and product development and assesses management's representations regarding the organization's compliance with environmental, health, and safety laws. The board monitors environmental management system improvements, ensuring that they are consistent with the organization's business management systems, goals, and objectives, and thus ensuring that the company meets the following conditions:

- A predictive, rather than reactive, management system is in place and thus the EMS becomes an enabler rather than an obstacle in bringing new projects or products on line on schedule, and the EMS contributes to growth and revenues.
- Environmental considerations are effectively factored into strategic, financial, and capital planning (for example, potential tax and other benefits are recognized at the planning stage).
- Effective, efficient, and consistent EHS management systems and processes are in place throughout all operations worldwide, thus minimizing costs as well as environmental and business risks.

In most organizations, the board appoints an environmental committee from its members to address such issues. The role of the environmental committee, like that of the full board, of course varies from organization to organization, but often its primary focus is on the following duties:

Directing EHS policy. Together with the chief executive officer, the board develops a meaningful mission statement that includes the organization's philosophy and approach to environmental responsibility. The board normally appoints a person from management to serve as chief environmental officer, or some similar title. This person has the responsibility for implementing the environmental management system with the goal of ensuring full conformance to corporate policies and strategic environmental objectives.

Reviewing EHS progress. The board periodically (no less frequently than annually) reviews the environmental progress of its organization, including major elements of the EMS, to ensure that all management systems are functioning as intended. The board reviews EMS audit reports generated by management or periodically commissions an outside review of the organization's environmental or EHS functions. The board is apprised of new developments, trends, and initiatives within the full spectrum of environmental management and reevaluates its organizational needs and responsibilities in light of those new or emerging developments.

Directing a corporate communication strategy. The board prepares an appropriate communications strategy for both internal and external audiences. More organizations are now preparing detailed environmental performance reports for distribution not only to shareholders but also to a broader audience of external stakeholders ("interested parties" in the language of ISO 14000). In light of increased interest in organizations' environmental matters, the board must be able to assure itself that the disseminated information is appropriate, accurate, and presented in a forthright and responsible fashion.

2.4   Conclusion

The early 1990s saw an end to the era of rapid-fire major federal environmental legislation and began a period of new opportunities for corporations to address their environmental responsibilities. The maturing of voluntary approaches to corporate environmental accountability and stewardship have evolved rapidly since 1990. This is in no small part due to the greater influence of customers, suppliers, investors, and other stakeholders locally, nationally, and globally, and to the availability of nationally and internationally accepted codes of practice, management principles, and formal management system approaches.

CHAPTER 3

VISION, VALUES, AND LEADERSHIP

If you don't know where you are going, any road will take you there.

ANONYMOUS

The values and guiding principles of companies, both implicit and explicit, form its corporate culture—and its culture, in turn, shapes and directs the efforts of its managers and workers. A company's culture determines the extent to which its stated values, principles, and policies are employed at critical decision-making junctions and, in fact, in everyday routine decisions. Culture influences the extent to which corporate policies and principles are translated into actions during all life-cycle stages of that corporation's projects, products, and services. It affects both formal and informal reward systems, communication methods, information management, and the company's relationship to its customers and other interested parties. Culture, then, becomes an essential determinant in aligning behaviors to produce desired results.

Anyone who has held a position with more than one company can attest that each has a unique culture, even within the same industry or business sector. In larger companies, different divisions or business units will have distinct cultures, especially where there has been a prevalence of merger and acquisition activity. In most companies, the norms and rules of this corporate culture are primarily learned through observation and on-the-job experience. In the best companies, the formal training, written policies, stated values, and leadership examples reinforce these informal, but real-life, learning experiences. We know that it takes no time at all for a new employee to evaluate the culture of the company that he or she has just joined and to spot disconnects between stated policies and actual or expected behaviors. These disconnects are real threats to the attainment of business goals.

3.1   The Vision Thing

In business, as with much of life, everything starts with a *vision*—a vision of where you are now and where you want to be in the future. Countless companies stumble at implementing detailed policies and otherwise well-thought-out strategic plans because their management does not share a common vision or downplays the role of a unifying vision in the company's success. Appropriate adages, both modern and ancient, that speak to this effect abound:

> *Where there is no vision, the people perish.*
>
> *Proverbs 29:18a*

> *Good business leaders create a vision, articulate the vision, passionately own the vision, and relentlessly drive it to completion.*
>
> *Jack Welch*
> *CEO, General Electric*

Vision itself may be a concept that is sometimes difficult to succinctly define, but history provides numerous examples of the consequences of the

---

3M is moving from a compliance-based system to one aimed at sustainability—producing more with fewer resources and less environmental impact. This means we must continue improving the way we design, make, and service products for our customers. 3M's Environmental Management System will help us identify opportunities. But, the innovation and dedication needed to contribute to sustainability must come from each of us. I am confident that together we will meet 3M's environmental goals and help our customers and society meet theirs.

L. D. DeSimone
3M Chairman and Chief Executive Officer

---

lack of a well-defined and -articulated vision among our elected leaders and appointed officials. Not surprisingly, in a corporate setting as well as in politics, vision often emanates from a single strong leader, such as GE's Welch, Monsanto's Robert Shapiro, or the late Roberto Goizueta, CEO of Coca-Cola, the global soft drink industry leader.

In 1997, for the second year in a row, *Fortune* magazine named Coca-Cola America's most admired company and also crowned it the *world's* most admired company. Much of Coca-Cola's success is credited to Cuban-born Goizueta's personal business vision and his long-term strategy for this successful beverage maker, whose product is frankly not all that different from its competitors' products. Some of Goizueta's business strategies were deceptively simple: Lower the company's cost of capital, divest underperforming business units, and reward performance. When Goizueta started his tenure as CEO, Coca-Cola was a dismal underperformer itself and was losing ground to its rival Pepsi in many markets. Its serious internal problems included poor communications and a culture of arrogance. When Goizueta passed away in October 1997, his visions and strategies had raised Coca-Cola's market value from a lackluster $4.3 billion to an impressive-by-any-standards $180 billion. And he changed the company's culture dramatically along the way.

Companies rise to prominence based upon leadership and the associated *vision,* however defined, or they flounder in mediocrity due at least in part to the lack of a defining vision. But to fully affect the company to the positive, the

---

We recognize the global nature of environmental, health, and safety issues, and our responsibilities to our employees, customers, and the communities in which we operate.... we are translating this recognition into tangible results through our management strategy, operations, and products. Digital is creating smart solutions for EHS issues through our practices and policies, our collaboration with business partners and research institutions, and our continuing excellence in information technology.

Robert B. Palmer
Chairman of the Board and Chief Executive Officer
Digital Equipment Corporation

> Our primary challenge ahead is to translate our EHS excellence into benefits for our shareholders, customers, communities, and employees.
>
> *William J. Post*
> *President and Chief Executive Officer*
> *Arizona Public Service Company*

vision must become a *shared vision;* it must become a part of the corporate culture that is understood, accepted, and embraced by the entire company. Ultimately, the corporate vision molds and influences the corporate *culture* and the *shared values,* and leads to the establishment of mission-critical strategies and policies that provide the opportunities for future success or failure.

This concept of shared values will define the character of the company. As Coca-Cola's Goizueta said:

> *Employees with integrity are the ones who build a company's reputation. Working for the Coca-Cola company is a calling. It's not a way to make a living. It's a religion.*
>
> Fortune, *March 3, 1997*

In *Fortune's* 1998 ranking, GE edged out Coca-Cola (and Microsoft) as America's most admired company. The magazine gave the full credit to Jack

> Each of these examples proves that what is good for the environment can be good for business. Going forward, Bank America will continue its environmental focus on making today's opportunities available to future generations . . . We think our customers, shareholders, and employees—indeed, all who occupy this planet—expect and deserve nothing less.
>
> *David A. Coulter*
> *Chairman and Chief Executive Officer*
> *Bank of America*

[E]nvironmental regulations often appear to be enacted without any consideration of shareholder value. But remember: environmental regulations aim at driving pollution from our systems, and pollution is waste! So, if we approach environmental regulations intelligently, our compliance can help us improve our efficiency. Our goal—your goal—should be twofold: first, full compliance with environmental laws and regulations—nothing short of excellence in environmental performance; second, total recovery of environmental expenditures in return on investment.

Jack Creighton
President and CEO
Weyerhaeuser Company

Welsh, who has kept GE "huge, nimble and immensely profitable." Admiration of GE is tied to leadership—Welch's personal leadership, of course, but also the institutional leadership that infuses the firm's top management. Reportedly, GE spends up to $800 million annually on training and leadership development—and on tirelessly spreading the Welch vision for the firm. Another well-quoted Jack Welch pronouncement speaks to the fervor that the GE vision represents:

Making your numbers but not demonstrating our values is grounds for dismissal.

Fortune, *October 27, 1997*

Of course, with the performance-driven Welch at the long-term helm of GE, *not* making your numbers understandably has its own consequences for a man-

[P]ollution prevention starts between the ears and the most critical ears belong to the CEO.

Denny J. Beroiz—1992
Director, Environmental Resource Management
B-2 Division, Northrop

> Achieving environmental, health, and safety excellence is part of an on-going process of continuous improvement involving all aspects of our business.
>
> *George A. Lorch*
> *Chairman and CEO*
> *Armstrong World Industries*

ager's career. Vision and values do not exist in a vacuum—they must eventually translate to performance and delivery. But if a company does not share a common vision, divergent strategies and dissimilar performance measurement systems will prevail—making the full attainment of corporate goals difficult, at best.

The highlighted quotes in this section illustrate the individual visions of nine corporate leaders whose companies have demonstrated environmental leadership in one or more areas. The companies these CEOs lead are not held up as perfect—measured either by economic performance, social accountability, or environmental stewardship—but they do represent a sound and clear vision expressed by an earnest leadership.

Leadership is undeniably the starting point. Leadership vision leads to organizational values, which lead to strategy. In the realm of environmental responsibility, they interlock with the principles of quality to compose an integrated management system that a company can use to establish itself as *best-in-class* among its peers.

> As Sun's new President, I have communicated my philosophy that health, environment, and safety (HES) performance goes hand-in-hand with operating reliability and financial success. Since 1997 is a pivotal year for Sun from a financial perspective, I consider our performance in HES to be one of our critical success factors.
>
> *John G. Drosdick*
> *President and Chief Operating Officer*
> *Sun Company, Inc.*

> Sustainable development means casting a wide net around resources, products and people and accounting for that system. Sustainable development is a journey rather than a destination.... Remember, leadership, environmental or otherwise, is the only ship that does not pull into a safe port in a storm.
>
> *Ted Boswell*
> *President*
> *The E. B. Eddy Group*

Leadership companies are attentive to their corporate cultural value systems and seek to have those values reflected through the implementation of their policies, procedures, strategies, and systems, realizing that environmental performance can affect business results. This environmental vision and leadership leads to establishing *values* and *guiding principles* that reflect a company's vision. These characteristics, in turn, direct the company's strategies and policies, which can be implemented through management systems (Figure 3.1).

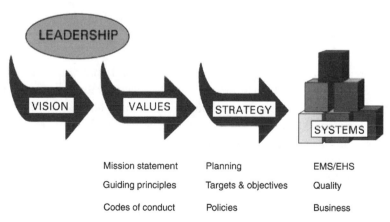

FIGURE 3.1. Leadership leads to a vision, values, and strategies that form the building blocks of a company's management systems.

3.2   Values and Principles

Formal mission statements and guiding principles highlight a company's values.

3.2.1   The Role of the Mission Statement

A corporate vision is most often reflected through its mission statement. A good mission statement expresses the vision, shared values, and overarching strategies of the organization and sets a course by which the company will steer. It is a critical corporate tool, a mechanism for self declaration and public proclamation.

Patricia Jones and Larry Kahaner express it this way in their 1995 book on corporate mission statements, *Say It And Live It:*

> *Corporate mission statements are manifestos; they outline in specific terms who we aspire to be and how we intend to realize our corporate aims. No other document—annual report, press release, news article, or statement from the board of directors—reveals more about a company's values and ethics than a mission statement. It is a map for the high road.*
>
> *A corporate mission statement is the most powerful tool a company has to implement change. The most effective way to ensure that all employees of either a global corporation or a small business understand the goals of the organization is to write a mission statement that leaves no doubt in anyone's mind.*

Mission statements that are not well thought out, do not truly reflect the values and sentiments of the company, or are just platitudinous phrases strung together can harm the company and hinder its chances for success. Employees, suppliers, and customers quickly realize that the mission statement is simply a document that hangs on the reception area wall but is devoid of any real connection to the organization they know.

The majority of published corporate mission statements focus on the company's overall core values and commonly include statements concerning its customer focus, continuous improvement, shareholder value, employee well-being, market leadership, and so forth. Such focus is understandable. Increasingly though, mission statements also reflect an outward view of greater social responsibility, and many progressive companies now include the concept of environmental stewardship in their statements. Noteworthy examples include the Georgia-Pacific (G-P) Corporation, a 70-year-old forest products company headquartered in Atlanta, and the venerable consumer manufacturer Gillette Company, headquartered in Boston. Both companies are highly visible to consumers and the public through their products and their widely dispersed manufacturing operations.

G-P's 1997 revenues were $13 billion, ranking it 116 on the Fortune 500 listing with 46,500 employees in more than 400 domestic facilities. G-P's corporate mission statement reflects the concept of doing the "right things," which includes promoting environmental stewardship through "assur[ing] leadership in its environmental performance and applying leading technology and scientific information to environmental solutions." This driving concept of doing the right things emanates from the leadership philosophy of its chairman and CEO, A. D. "Pete" Correll. In a heavy manufacturing industry sector with significant large-volume material, waste handling, and emission issues, Correll has set the standard for making environmental performance and safety performance top priorities at G-P.

In describing its corporate values, Gillette expresses its approach to good citizenship:

> We will comply with applicable laws and regulations at all government levels wherever we do business. We will contribute to the communities in which we operate and address social issues responsibly. Our products will be safe to make and use. We will conserve natural resources, and we will continue to invest in a better environment.

Like G-P's Pete Correll, Gillette's CEO, Alfred Zeien, has been a visible leader for environmental responsibility.

These two examples, though quite different and certainly tailored for their respective companies, reflect a public commitment at the most senior levels. They present the corporate *vision* clearly and prominently and set the tone for corporate values and culture to follow to reflect that vision. Neither statement is lengthy or flowery, but within these organizations environmental strategy is acknowledged as a "party at the table"—a corporate core value that seeks opportunity to be fully integrated with the wide range of already recognized business values.

The best of the mission statements, especially when a company's business climate is changing and it must reevaluate its direction, address such critical factors as the following:

- What is our reason for being in business?
- What products or service lines should we be continuing or entering?
- Where do we want the company to be in 5 years? 10 years?
- What are the critical success factors that will determine our success?

All too often, corporate mission statements are justifiably ripe for criticism by employees and external stakeholders. Why? They often are as follows:

- *Unfocused.* Many mission statements try to be so encompassing and generalized that they could apply to almost any organization. The written statements are vague and rely heavily on the use of current business buzzwords.
- *Unconnected.* Do the words of the mission statement reflect the company culture and mission as understood by all affected parties? Conflicting goals embodied in other corporate documents or policies will, at best, put a tarnish on the mission statement's impact, and at worst will lead to serious confusion affecting multiple layers of the company.
- *Insincere.* Or at least they have the tone of insincerity. Does management "walk the walk," or are these just words on paper? In times of business downturns and restructuring, do corporate actions reflect the printed statements on the "value of our talented work force" that is "our most important asset"?

In the arena of environmental responsibility, such characteristics as those just presented are deadly. Increasingly, employees and stakeholders take environment responsibility issues seriously and expect the companies they work for, buy from, and invest in to be just as serious and to accept their leadership position. Many corporations, large and small, do. The mission statement then sets the stage for the subsequent and supporting efforts of environmental strategy, policy development, and management systems creation and integration.

As will be seen later in this chapter and especially in Chapter 5, the company's vision of its environmental performance goals is critical to the development of an EMS's environmental policy and actually is the primary driver for an effective EMS.

3.2.2 Guiding Principles

Many companies formally adopt sets of internal guiding principles, corporate values, statements of beliefs, or codes of conduct—statements of corporate character and expectations for all employees. Most often these statements go beyond the broader corporate mission statement in addressing key values and characteristics that the company professes to hold. Even the best guiding principles do not necessarily address specific targets and goals but are more likely to specify desirable attributes that lead to, and support, environmental goals and strategies.

Guiding principles most commonly do the following:

- Describe key characteristics of the present, and future, company culture.

Fundamental to our success are the values we believe and practice.

People are the source of our success. We treat one another with respect, promote teamwork and encourage personal freedom and growth. Leadership and excellence in performance are sought and rewarded.

Customers are the reason we exist. They receive our strongest commitment to meet their needs.

Our *products* and *services* reflect dedication to quality, innovation and value.

Our *conduct* demonstrates integrity and commitment to ethics, safety, health and the environment.

Dow Values
The Dow Chemical Company

- Present succinct and powerful statements that define how management and workers are expected to conduct their job-related activities.
- Align with and support the company's mission statement and goals, objectives, targets, and identified critical success factors.

The preceding and following examples, from two manufacturing companies on opposite ends of the size spectrum, reflect both human resource and environmental values that are deeply held.

We believe that both human beings and nature have inherent worth and deserve our respect.

We believe in products that are safe, effective, and made of natural ingredients.

We believe that our company and our products are unique and worthwhile, and that we can sustain these genuine qualities with an ongoing commitment to innovation and creativity.

We believe that we have a responsibility to cultivate the best relationships possible with our co-workers, customers, owners, agents, suppliers and our community.

We believe that different people bring different gifts and perspectives to the team and that a strong team is founded on a variety of gifts.

We believe in providing employees with a safe and fulfilling work environment, and an opportunity to grow and learn.

We believe that competence is an essential means of sustaining our values in a competitive marketplace.

We believe our company can be financially successful while behaving in a socially responsible and environmentally sensitive manner.

Statement of Beliefs
Tom's of Maine

With an understanding of its vision and core values, a company is well on the road to establishing a workable, detailed strategy and complementary environmental policies.

3.3 Environmental Strategy

A strategy is essentially an integrated set of actions that supports the enactment of the company's long-term vision, values, and objectives. Strategy becomes the vehicle that links the lofty corporate mission statement to a delivery system; in this case, strategy links the environmental management system with its counterparts in quality and business management systems. Strategy provides a critical piece of the integrated systems puzzle (Figure 3.2).

While the ultimate corporate vision may be the product of the senior management team, or even of a sole leader, as we've seen, establishing a strategy as practiced in leading corporations is much more of an inclusive effort involving managers and workers at multiple levels. Long gone are the mammoth central strategic planning departments like the one dismantled by Jack Welch at GE in 1983. Also, unlike the much discredited strategic planning band-

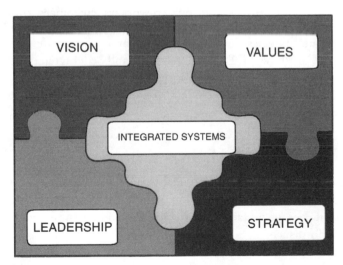

FIGURE 3.2. The components of an integrated EHS system.

wagon of the late 1970s and early 1980s, such planning today has a decidedly outward focus, reflecting customer-driven ideas and opportunities, the reality of global competition, and the need to address a wide spectrum of stakeholder concerns. It also seeks to establish clear value propositions and the necessary resources required to fulfill the strategic plan.

The process of setting a strategy, within the context of environmental, health, and safety issues, usually involves several key components:

- The strategic planning process itself—the suitable scope of the effort and who will participate.
- Setting broad targets and objectives for the company that build upon the mission statement and other corporate goals. Strategic planning should result in a series of specific action items with responsibilities for their execution.
- Establishing the overall environmental or EHS policy that supports the corporate vision and objectives.
- Determining which, if any, industry codes of practice or other external management principles will be adopted by the company (Responsible Care, STEP, CERES, ICC charter, etc.).
- Determining the nature of the environmental management system (or EHS management system) suitable to implement the stated corporate strategies (ISO 14001, EMAS, or a company-developed system) and how this EMS will relate to, and be integrated with, existing or planned management systems to add value.
- Establishing a framework for a communication strategy, both internally and externally.

3.4 Environmental Policy

At its core, a company's environmental policy is an opportunity to state its principles and future intentions and provide a framework for developing supportive strategies, goals, targets, and objectives and measurement of environmental performance.

Corporate environmental policies have evolved considerably over the past ten years, having been influenced by inclusion of the issue in corporate mission statements, the Total Quality Management movement of the 1980s, and the formalization of EMS approaches in the 1990s through BS 7750 and ISO 14001. Early policies were often a component of a corporate quality statement or were simple and brief declarations generated within the environmental department EHS functional unit. The best policies are now linked to a strong corporate mission statement and express the integrated approach of the company to environmental management.

Chapter 5.1 discusses environmental policy in the context of the EMS development process. Here, however, we want to explore some of the general concepts common to most environmental policies and the strategies that drive those policies.

No single published checklist of items to include within an environmental policy would necessarily suffice for all organizations. ISO 14001 and the companion ISO 14004 certainly suggest many issues for consideration. Others are found within the Total Quality Environmental Management (TQEM) approach espoused by GEMI and other organizations. But the characteristics exhibited by some of the better published statements reflect the following points:

- *Relevancy.* Policies are tied to the corporate mission statement and reflect the company's policies and guiding principles.
- *Commitment.* Policies express a commitment to environmental excellence that goes beyond meeting only minimum regulatory requirements.
- *Stewardship.* Policies reflect an outward view and an acceptance of responsibility for stewardship that goes beyond traditional corporate boundaries. The concerns of local and regional interested parties are considered.
- *Integration.* Policies coordinate with or integrate with other organizational functions, goals, and strategies and with core business functions.
- *Communication.* The vision for environmental excellence is shared internally and externally and views from within and outside the company are sought.

An example of a relatively brief environmental policy statement that forms the framework for subsequent initiatives, goals, and objectives was developed by

Baxter International, Inc. (discussed in detail in Chapter 5.1). Baxter has seven succinct policy statements that describe its commitments in the following areas:

- Sustainable development
- Compliance
- Customers
- Employees
- Suppliers and contractors
- Community and government
- Business integration

Baxter then proceeds to tie its environmental progress reporting to these seven commitments in detailed and quantitative sections of its annual published performance report.

As another example of a well-developed approach, the Georgia-Pacific Corporation developed 18 extensive principles that establish its environmental and safety objectives. These principles are grouped into four major categories:

- **Management Focus**—These principles reflect our expectations of how we will manage our company to ensure we are meeting our environmental and safety responsibilities.
- **Conservation and Sustainable Use of Resources**—This category of principles will guide us in managing the forests and other natural resources we need to manufacture our products so that there will be resources for future generations.
- **Protection of Health and the Environment**—This section outlines our continuing commitment to the health and safety of our employees, our communities and our environment.
- **Promote Community Awareness**—These principles map out the responsibility of Georgia-Pacific operations to be active participants in our communities and to communicate on environmental and safety issues.

Georgia-Pacific's principles are supported by measurable goals, which are established with the participation of its employees.

A somewhat different approach to a policy statement is taken by the ICI Group of the United Kingdom, a diversified chemical company with worldwide manufacturing and retail operations. ICI has strengthened its safety, health, and environment (SHE) policies in recent years, as reflected in its lengthy corporate policy statement:

> *The ICI Group will ensure that all its activities world-wide are conducted safely; the health of its employees, its customers and the public will be protected; environmental performance will meet contemporary requirements, and that its operations are run in a manner acceptable to the local community.*
>
> *In particular we will:*
>
> *Comply with the relevant laws and regulations and take any additional measures we consider necessary.*
>
> *Ensure that all our activities are being carried out in accordance with the ICI Group Safety, Health and Environmental Standards. .*
>
> *Set demanding targets and measure progress to ensure continuous improvement in safety, health and environmental performance.*
>
> *Require every member of staff to exercise personal responsibility in preventing harm to themselves, others and the environment, and enable them to contribute to every aspect of safety, health and environmental protection.*
>
> *Manufacture only those products that can be transported, stored, used and disposed of safely.*
>
> *Seek to develop new or modified products which assist in conserving the environment and lead to sustainable development.*
>
> *Provide appropriate safety, health and environment training and information for all our staff, contractors and others who work with us, handle our products, or operate our technologies.*
>
> *Communicate openly on the nature of our activities and report progress on our safety, health and environmental performance.*
>
> *Promote the interchange of safety, health and environmental information and technology throughout the ICI Group and make our expertise and knowledge available to relevant statutory authorities.*
>
> *Encourage, through positive interaction with the industry, the world-wide development and implementation of the principles of the Chemical Industries' "Responsible Care®" initiative and the International Chamber of Commerce's "Business Charter for Sustainable Development".*

Three aspects of the ICI SHE policy statement that reflect areas of strong emphasis within the company are worth further comment.

Worker safety.   Traditionally, ICI has maintained a strong focus on safety and this is reflected by the emphasis given this issue in its annual SHE performance reports. However, the focus on the environmental component of the SHE policy has been increased in recent years.

Manufacturing controls.   Within the ICI family of companies is ICI Paints North America, headquartered in Cleveland. ICI Paints has developed computer programs that control the formulation of all of its products. All paint components have been evaluated for toxicity characteristics and handling and disposal requirements in their intended formulations. The controlling computer system will not allow the formulation of out-of-spec products, thereby preventing the unintentional creation of a handling or disposal issue not previously addressed by the SHE groups. This system is being evaluated for application within all of the ICI operating businesses.

Information and technology exchange.   A corporate SHE council provides a forum for discussing issues critical to all ICI business groups and maximizing the available resources.

Taken together, ICI's SHE policy sets the framework for developing business group–specific strategies, goals, targets, and objectives that are consistent with corporate core values. A strong SHE policy allows for the smooth integration of new acquisitions into the ICI system, such as occurred in mid-1996 with the National Starch and Chemical Company and several other entities.

3.5   Conclusion

As the brief examples in this chapter have illustrated, vision, values, and leadership work together to support strong environmental policy and strategy development. This sequencing of supportive activities provides companies with a clear sense of direction and the ability to accomplish meaningful and documentable environmental performance improvements through its EMS and associated management systems. These key elements combined form the integrated system.

SECTION II

THE ENVIRONMENTAL MANAGEMENT SYSTEM (EMS) APPROACH

Chapters 4 through 8 discuss in some detail the framework of an EMS. They provide a basic level of understanding of the essential elements of an EMS and of how to plan and implement an EMS. They are not written to be a workbook for EMS implementation. They will, however, walk you through the steps you must follow to develop and implement an EMS for your company. This section relies on the experiences of companies who have already been through the process to provide examples of how your company might approach each EMS element. Chapter 9 closes this section by providing an in-depth look at environmental performance measurement and reporting.

CHAPTER 4

ENVIRONMENTAL MANAGEMENT SYSTEMS

Environmental management system—the part of the overall management system that includes organizational structure, planning activities, responsibilities, practices, procedures, processes and resources for developing, implementing, achieving, reviewing and maintaining the environmental policy.

DEFINITION 3.5
ISO 14001:1996

This chapter takes a look at the environmental management system (EMS), focusing on the basic concepts, benefits to your company, and the necessary steps to plan and implement an EMS. For many years, companies have in many ways kept environmental issues separated from other business management functions. Corporate environmental managers have responded to crises. Their interaction with plant or process personnel has typically been, at worst, in the realm of enforcement or, at best, in providing a resource for help to those personnel in areas they view as necessary evils or unwanted bureaucracy. This situation has been perpetuated, if not created, in the United States by the nature of command-and-control regulation at both the state and federal levels. As discussed in the first part of this book, command-and-control regulation has resulted in significant advancements in the state of the environment, but the costs have been high and an environmental bureaucracy of significant proportions has resulted. As has been seen, both regulators and companies have come to recognize that a more cooperative relationship between regulators and regulated companies can be more cost-effective and still provide environmental improvement. Likewise, better proactive management of environmental aspects can reduce environmental costs.

4.1   Why Companies Care about an EMS

Managers frequently ask why they should develop an EMS. It's just one more set of headaches, more distraction from the "real" business of running their operations and making a profit. In their previous book, *The ISO 14000 Answer Book,* written for business managers, the authors suggest that the better question is: Why not develop an EMS? Companies have developed systems to better manage their employees, their accounting and cash flow, their marketing, and their quality assurance. Each of these systems has a cost associated with its development and implementation. However, these costs are offset by benefits in terms of efficiency, increased market share, or decreased overall operating costs.

Environmental liability is one of the biggest potential cash drains on a business. Viewed for so long as an unpleasant cost of doing business, a reactionary mode for dealing with environmental issues has developed. Certainly, aggressive command-and-control regulations have fueled this reactionary approach. Doing what it takes to stay out of trouble can be a full-time job. What the reactionary approach does not encourage is creative thinking aimed at developing cost-effective approaches to dealing with environmental issues. Nevertheless, if a company could develop a process to understand and handle its environmental issues in a more cost-effective manner, potentially identifying operational processes or approaches that are innovative and provide cost benefits to the company, would it not try to develop such a process? The rising interest in the EMS as a management tool is based on the prospect that proactive environmental management may provide just those benefits.

There are a number of driving forces fueling the growing interest in the EMS. Regulators at both the state and federal levels are showing increased interest in the use of the EMS as a way to create better cooperation between regulators and the regulated community. The end, or even significant reduction, of command-and-control regulations is not likely to occur in the foreseeable future. However, EPA has recognized the potential of the EMS in its Project XL, Environmental Leadership Program (ELP), and Common Sense Initiatives. Likewise, similar interest in the EMS can be seen at the federal level in terms of penalty reduction and mitigation and of approaches to regulatory oversight and permitting. One only need look at the EPA audit policy or the U.S. Sentencing Guidelines. EPA regional initiatives have created joint state-EPA programs aimed at providing companies with information and assistance on understanding the value of an EMS and guidance for planning and implementing an EMS. Likewise, numerous initiatives are being put forth independently by various states that use the EMS approach as a means of reducing the degree of oversight or the complexity of the permit process.

Customer demands provide another driving force. The development of EMS standards at the international level, such as ISO 14000 or the Eco-Management and Audit Scheme (EMAS), have resulted in a market where suppliers of goods or services are increasingly expected to have EMS certifications.[1] The customers for your goods or services may require an EMS certification as a part of product specification. Growing acceptance or recognition of the value placed on EMS certification may result in a market where being able to demonstrate compliance with EMS principles provides a significant advantage. The growth and acceptance of quality management systems (QMS), even before ISO 9000, created a situation where companies touted their QMS as a means of gaining market advantage. Whether companies decide to certify under a particular EMS standard, self-declare under an EMS standard, or implement an EMS independent of any standard, market advantage, as driven by customer demand, will play an important role in that decision-making process.

Finally, cost savings and decreased liability provide additional driving forces. As with any other function of your business, better efficiency and better planning result in lower costs to get your product or service to your customers. The quantitative impact of an EMS cannot be measured until implementation and practical use provide the necessary data. At the least, however, it seems clear that having an EMS in place can, in many cases, result in decreased civil penalties and criminal liabilities. As a best case, having an EMS in place has the potential to provide proactive identification of environmental problems (resulting in fewer regulatory penalties and less negative publicity), to identify opportunities to avoid environmental liability (waste minimization, selection of raw materials with fewer environmental impacts, and better employee awareness), and to provide better company image and increased market share.

As mentioned in Chapter 1, Americas Materials Recovery Operation (AMRO), a small to medium-sized subsidiary of Digital Equipment Corporation, made an early commitment to developing an EMS and seeking ISO 14001 certification. For AMRO, ISO 14001 certification was based on three primary factors: business leadership, customer relationships and marketplace differentiation, and a positive experience with ISO 9000 implementation.

Ford Motor Company of Canada believed that ISO 14001 conformed well with other management systems already in place. It has a corporate certificate for an ISO 9001 quality management system. In making a business decision to seek ISO 14001 implementation and certification, Ford Canada recognized the following motivations:

- Public interest
- Consistency with business strategy
- Consistency with environmental strategy
- Commercial necessity
- Commercial advantage
- Cost reduction
- Increased effectiveness and efficiency

In the services area, the Hong Kong Island Shangri-La hotel recognized as early as 1993 the impact that a large hotel could have on the environment. The Island Shangri-La developed an environmental policy document, which resulted in the identification and implementation of environmentally related best practices. Therefore, it was no surprise that the hotel joined the first EMS pilot program in Asia in 1995 and ultimately achieved ISO 14001 certification.

Likewise, the Copley Square Hotel in Boston understands the significance of environmental performance for a hotel located in a historic location and which caters to a top-market clientele. This recognition of the value of good environmental performance has resulted in an aggressive program to identify and reduce its environmental impact.

4.2 How Companies Benefit from an EMS

In its simplest terms, an EMS is a systematic approach to dealing with the environmental aspects of a company's business. It is not something new or unique. Many companies have had several of the elements that make up an EMS in place for years. In the United States, environmental regulations require many of the elements of an EMS in some form or other. These include the development of operational procedures, training, audits, corrective action, or emergency preparedness. The concept of an EMS brings together a number of elements in a framework which provides for coordination of the various elements and allows management to systematically understand and control the many components of environmental management. An important part of the EMS is to track how the various parts of the EMS are functioning so that management can make corrections and take the actions necessary to prevent future problems. An EMS may be implemented across an entire company, but it may also be implemented individually in each division or at each plant.

An EMS is meant to provide control over a company's *environmental aspects*. This notion of aspects is key. An environmental aspect is any activity of a company that has a negative or positive impact on the environment. As is discussed later, the EMS is developed on the basis of what significant environmental aspects the particular company has identified. Clearly, some companies have many environmental aspects, whereas small or medium enterprises (SMEs) often have very few environmental aspects. An EMS should provide understanding and control of these environmental aspects, and can lead to overall environmental improvement as a result of better control.

Since an EMS mainly provides formalization of procedures that often already exist, it is important to make use of the information or processes that are already in place. Development of an EMS does not require a complete retooling of your environmental management. It should take better advantage of and make better use of as much existing information as possible. Companies are required to collect considerable data as part of their regulatory requirements. Outside of an EMS, these data are likely collected, stored, and reported to the appropriate regulator. That same data, however, can also provide significant informational input to the EMS.

For example, a company reports total pounds of air emissions per year to the regulator. That same data, when correlated with production data, can be used within an EMS to provide an indicator of the environmental efficiency of a process. That is, it can provide management with the pounds of air emission per unit of product produced. This may be important to management if one of the goals of the EMS is to reduce overall air emissions. No new data is needed, and the use of the data for a specific purpose within the EMS is easy. As will be seen later, as the EMS is developed, based on the environmental aspects and the goals set for the EMS, much of the information needed to implement the EMS may already be available and may require only minimal reevaluation.

An EMS, then, is a process to assist management in dealing with the significant environmental aspects of the business. This is a broader view than just compliance with regulations and addresses many potential environmental impacts that are not regulated (e.g., energy and natural resources). Through development of awareness of those aspects, taking information or data from throughout the operational processes, and tracking the performance of developed procedures, the EMS provides management with a tool to understand and control the business' environmental aspects in a systematic and continuing manner.

As a result, an EMS can lead to numerous organizational and financial benefits. The systematic approach to consideration of environmental impacts, the awareness created at all levels of the organization, and the empowerment of individual employees to control their incremental contribution to the company's environmental performance all provide a foundation upon which countless benefits may accrue. Wilton Armetale is an SME foundry located in Pennsylvania. Wilton's ISO 14001 EMS has resulted in benefits such as the following:

- Better employee understanding of waste handling procedures
- A reduction in waste generation by employees
- A better relationship with the state environmental regulators
- Improved community relationships

Although these benefits may not have readily quantifiable costs associated with them, the overall positive impact on the company will translate to financial gain. AMRO's EMS has resulted in a better understanding of material flow through the facility and an increased awareness of the opportunities to reclaim or recycle components that perhaps were not previously identified for reuse. In a business whose bottom line is directly tied to the ability to take obsolete equipment and turn a profit by the creative reuse of component parts, increased awareness translates directly to profits.

Key areas of financial benefit have also resulted from initiatives and programs related to waste minimization and pollution prevention. One might argue that it does not require an EMS to achieve these benefits. The importance of the EMS is in its ability to focus on a broad-based understanding of a company's environmental aspects and impacts and to provide a mechanism for more easily identifying opportunities for waste minimization and pollution prevention. By its nature, an EMS creates an organizational atmosphere which not only makes identification of opportunities more likely, but actually encourages the creative searching out of opportunities.

There appears to be little remaining doubt as to the potential for an EMS to result in financial benefits, and examples are plentiful. Wilton reported a 60-percent decrease in solid waste volumes and costs, while production rates increased. Copley Square Hotel has reported annual electrical savings of over $6,000 due to energy efficiency programs, annual savings of over $13,000 due to water use reduction programs, and savings of over $4,000 annually due to recycling programs. Finally, Wolstenholme International, a medium-sized English manufacturer of pigments and inks, reported savings of $162,000 due to EMS implementation in areas of energy and raw material consumption.

4.3 Essential Elements of an EMS

There have been several models for EMS at the international level, including EMAS, ISO 14001/14004, and BS 7750 (which formed the early basis for ISO 14001 and is now all but subsumed by ISO 14001). All of these standards are very similar in approach, varying mainly in their specific requirements on specific issues. The discussion which follows does not try to include specific elements of any particular EMS standard, but addresses in a general fashion a set of essential elements basic to any systematic approach to environmental management. Most EMS models borrow from the Total Quality Management (TQM) concept of Plan-Do-Check-Act, resulting in a system that continually improves through repeating this cycle. In the case of EMS, this continual improvement should result in an overall improvement in environmental performance. However, an EMS need not require improvement in environmental performance; indeed ISO 14001 certification is not directly predicated upon a demonstration of improved environmental performance (although an EMS that does not lead to at least some improvement in environmental performance over time is arguably not functioning properly).

An EMS should not create a new level of bureaucracy for your company, but should be an integration of environmental issues into your mainstream business management functions. Existing management procedures and systems can often form the basis or framework for your EMS. For example, if you have management procedures in place to train employees, environmental training can be built into that program. If you have human resources procedures for developing and describing job descriptions, those procedures can merely be expanded to encompass specific requirements for environmentally sensitive work activities.

The approach is to put the environment into your business management; to create an overall management approach to identifying and controlling environmental impacts.

Therefore, your EMS must be just that—*your* EMS. It should reflect the way you do business, be sensitive to the type of business you conduct, reflect your company image or culture, and be responsive to your management and employees. To make an EMS company-specific, consider the following steps in the EMS development process:

Understand your EMS needs. The first step is to think hard about your company, the operations it performs, the products or services it provides, and the market it sells to. Determine what aspects of your business could benefit from a more systematic approach to environmental management. Decide what you are committed to do to better manage your environmental affairs.

Understand what aspects of your business impact upon the environment. Your EMS should specifically address some problem or set of problems that you need to solve. Otherwise, why waste time developing a system to control and solve problems? Therefore, you need to know how your business interacts with the environment, in both a positive and negative manner. You also need to define what the environmental impact is for each such aspect of your business. If your business had minimal or no interaction with the environment then you would not need an EMS. The degree of significant interaction with the environment that your company has defines the EMS that you need.

Decide how you want to address each environmental aspect of your business. You must develop a set of objectives that reflect which environmental aspects you consider most significant and address how you wish to exert control over those aspects. You cannot control or manage every environmental aspect of your business all at once. Therefore, you need to define a set of objectives which can reasonably be met in a designated time frame and which will exert a reasonable amount of control to bring about better management of your environmental impacts. As your EMS progresses, you can encompass more aspects by setting additional objectives, thus providing an ever-greater measure of management control.

Design your EMS to address the significant environmental aspects of your business. Your EMS should be designed to specifically address those significant environmental aspects of your business that you defined in the previous step. Your EMS should not be some boiler-plate management structure, but a management structure whose every element has a specific purpose toward achieving the defined objectives. Avoid wasting time and energy doing things that don't specifically improve your progress toward each objective.

Develop procedures to monitor the progress of your EMS. You must be able to monitor the progress you are making toward reaching each objective. Therefore, you need procedures to measure how well your EMS is functioning, compared to the objectives set by your management. This can be done by developing indicators to measure the performance of your EMS as well as environmental performance. These indicators must provide specific information in a format useful to understanding and measuring the effectiveness of your EMS. For example, if you have an objective of reducing energy consumption through energy efficiency projects, it is not very useful to measure total energy consumption over time. It is more meaningful to measure energy consumption over time as a ratio of the amount of product produced during that time.

It is important to remember that no packaged EMS exists for your company. An EMS is a process for managing the environmentally related elements of your business. Therefore, it must be fashioned to your specific needs and must be developed and implemented at a pace and in a manner that works for your type of business and your type of management approach.

The remainder of Section 4.3 will consider the essential elements of an EMS. This will form the basic understanding that will lead into Chapters 5, 6, and 7, which will discuss in detail how you can plan and implement an EMS for your company by learning from the experiences of companies who have already been through the process.

4.3.1   Ensuring Management Commitment

Effective implementation of an EMS will result in a cultural change in the way you and your employees view environmental performance. Therefore, it is critical that the decision to implement an EMS comes from top management and carries the total commitment of top management. Employees at all levels of the company must understand that environmental management is as fundamental to the company as financial management, production management, or any other key function of the company. Thinking about environmental management must be part of every facet of the company's and each employee's activities. When the design engineer starts working on a new process design, it must be second nature to her to be designing with environmental performance in mind. When the janitor cleans the production area, he must be thinking about environmental performance in the selection of cleaning products or the disposal of wastes. Such a cultural change cannot happen without strong leadership and obvious belief and commitment in the value of environmental management. The environmental policy is the public declaration of top management's commitment and the primary framework for planning and implementing the company's EMS.

4.3.2   Understanding the Company's Environmental Aspects and Other Requirements

As previously stated, an EMS starts with a commitment by senior management to develop a system for managing the company's impact on the environment. This commitment includes a serious consideration of the company's environmental aspects as the basis for determining what needs to be managed. The environmental aspects are any activities that can interact with the environment. This includes *negative aspects,* such as emissions, raw material consumption, energy consumption, and land use, as well as *beneficial aspects,* such as energy production (e.g., hydro power), environmentally friendly products, and recycling.

Before developing the EMS, a company also needs to understand the environmental requirements under which it operates. These may be legal requirements (state and federal regulations), industry practices, internal procedures, and the like. A company will need to establish goals and objectives for most legal requirements and may wish to establish them for other requirements as well. If there are corporate procedural requirements for audit frequency, for example, a particular plant or division will want to consider those in setting up its EMS. Each company will approach the EMS process differently, and it is critical to understand one's own requirements, of any type, that have a bearing on the functionality and success of the EMS.

4.3.3   Setting Goals and Objectives

The EMS needs a set of goals or objectives that management wants to achieve through implementation of the EMS. This very important step ensures that there is a clear understanding of the reasons for implementing the EMS and of the outputs or benefits that should be expected. Without clear goals and objectives, the EMS is merely a process in and of itself with no real benefit to the company. The environmental aspects form the foundation for the EMS goals and objectives, which should be directly related to the significant environmental aspects and the environmental policy.

The goals and objectives take the concepts of environmental performance established by the environmental policy, environmental aspects, and legal and other requirements and translate them into action items which can be understood and carried out by the employees (from management on down) of your company. These are your company-specific goals and objectives, and they must fit with the way your company operates and be capable of achieving your desired environmental performance.

4.3.4   Reviewing Existing Operations and Procedures

Once a company understands what it needs to manage (environmental aspects), what it wants to achieve from the EMS process (goals and objectives), and what environmental requirements it must consider, it needs to determine what shape it is in now. This is a review of its environmental management history, including compliance history, employee awareness of environmental issues, results of internal audits, and so forth. In the vernacular of ISO 14001 implementation (borrowed from ISO 9000 implementation), this is called *initial review and gap analysis*. See where you stand now and compare it to what you need to do to meet your goals and objectives.

Some view the initial review and gap analysis as a preliminary step to the entire EMS development process, occurring immediately after the completion of the environmental policy. The authors prefer to have some idea of the basic requirements of the EMS before the review, and to use the review as a preliminary step to developing the environmental management programs necessary to achieve the goals and objectives. In fact, it may be that some level of review is necessary at both points in the process. Certainly, you will need some knowledge of the current state of your company's environmental performance to understand your environmental aspects and set goals and objectives. A compliance audit, if one has not been conducted recently, is often a good way to identify legal requirements and gain insight into your environmental performance.

However, performing a gap analysis before you think through the basic requirements for your company's EMS, especially if conducted by an outside professional, may result in a lot of findings that are inappropriate to your specific interests or needs. Only you know your level of understanding of your environmental performance, and only you can determine the reviews necessary for your EMS development.

This step in the process has basic importance. The EMS will in many cases use existing information and will merely reformat it or use it in different ways than may have been contemplated in the past. Therefore, it is very important to understand what systems are already in place and how effective they are. When deciding later, during planning, how or what kind of data to collect, it is critical to understand opportunities to avoid reinventing the wheel or, equally bad, to avoid setting up procedures that are contrary to or interfere with existing adequate procedures. Change is sometimes necessary, but change only for change's sake is inefficiency at its worst.

4.3.5 Developing Environmental Management Programs

The environmental management programs are the mechanism by which the actions identified by the implementation team during planning are actually carried out. Whereas the implementation plan may set a milestone for some portion of your EMS planning or implementation to be completed, it is the environmental management programs that will ensure that the appropriate people and resources undertake the appropriate tasks to meet that milestone.

Environmental management programs are the guides that explain to employees what must be done and how it must be done. For example, if your company has an objective of reducing electrical consumption by 10 percent over the next 12 months, the environmental management program necessary for achieving the objective and target would spell out specific areas for improving the control of energy use. It may also describe energy efficiency initiatives to be implemented. The environmental management programs should be developed for discrete tasks or activities and should designate a person responsible for achieving the objectives and targets associated with those tasks or activities. Likewise, they should describe the available resources committed to completing those tasks or activities. Finally, they should set a time by which it is expected that the program(s) will be in place.

4.3.6   Implementing the EMS

Once it has established its existing conditions, a company is ready to begin the process of implementing the EMS. Implementing includes creating the framework for the EMS, assigning responsibilities, communicating essential EMS information, documenting EMS elements, and developing the necessary operational procedures to make the EMS function.

There are many courses being offered to assist companies with implementation of an EMS (most are aimed at ISO 14001). These courses may provide enough help to proceed with the process internally. Another approach is to hire a consultant to help at various points throughout the process, including initial strategy development; determining environmental aspects, goals, and objectives; performing initial reviews; and providing assistance during planning and implementation. The advantage of hiring a consultant to help is that your employees get on-the-job training and learn by doing.

The implementation process should also assign responsibilities at all levels of the company and ensure that appropriate communication mechanisms are in place to provide the necessary EMS information to the appropriate employees. Procedures, responsibilities, goals and objectives, and so forth should be documented both to provide ready reference to employees and to provide a baseline against which the EMS's performance can be judged. Finally, operational procedures may need to be developed or amended. What procedures are needed will depend on what procedures a company already has in place and the complexity of the company's operations.

4.3.7 Training Employees

Once the EMS procedures are developed, they must be explained to employees, without whose active participation and understanding the EMS cannot succeed. There are three types of training associated with implementation of an EMS: awareness training, EMS procedures training, and specific job training.

Awareness training is critical to the success of the EMS and should include all employees. Awareness training is used to ensure that all employees understand the environmental significance of the company's activities as well as their own individual activities. Employees need to understand that they have direct impact on whether the company meets the goals and objectives of the EMS.

EMS procedures training provides detailed instruction on the procedures necessary to implement and maintain the EMS, including individual responsibilities. Anyone who has any responsibilities under the EMS needs to understand what those responsibilities are and how they are to be carried out.

Specific job training involves those whose work activities have the most direct impact on the environment. These could include treatment plant operators, waste disposal personnel, or chemical buyers. The EMS relies on individuals performing critical tasks in an appropriate manner. Therefore, training is critical to ensure that employees are capable of performing those tasks.

4.3.8 Monitoring Performance

The EMS must include procedures for monitoring how well the goals and objectives established by the EMS are being met. This requires developing procedures for measuring the performance of specific elements of the EMS. These procedures may take the form of compliance audits (looking at compliance with external requirements), systems audits (looking at how the EMS is functioning as compared to what the EMS procedures require—is training occurring, are audits being performed, etc.), and establishing indicators that provide a measure of performance.

The complexity of the EMS will determine the number and types of monitoring procedures that are needed. Sufficient data are required to ensure that the EMS is operating as designed, is having the results anticipated, and has considered all significant environmental aspects.

4.3.9 Reviewing the EMS and Taking Corrective Action

The final element in an EMS is review and corrective action. Data obtained from procedures established for monitoring performance must be provided to management for review. This review is critical to determining whether the assumptions used in developing the EMS were correct and whether procedures developed to implement the EMS are adequate, overly bureaucratic, or provide unnecessary or wrong direction. Based on the analysis of this review, steps must be taken to correct deficiencies and adjust the system to obtain the desired performance. Since an EMS is an ongoing process, this continuing measurement and review provides management with the information needed to improve the system. The ultimate goal is an EMS that provides management with the best tools necessary to control the environmental aspects of its operations in as cost-effective a manner as possible.

CHAPTER 5

PLANNING YOUR COMPANY'S EMS

Like anything else, a good EMS requires good planning. The tendency exists to grab the ISO 14000 standards and start trying to implement the various elements, perhaps even hiring consultants to immediately begin working with your plant personnel. Likewise, the *gap analysis* has become the de facto first step toward EMS implementation. It is an easy start because there are many consultants waiting to provide your company with a gap analysis, and it is a step you can take without much thought and with reasonably limited resources. Unfortunately, it can frequently be a waste of resources.

The value of a review of your existing environmental programs before you start making changes to your operations cannot be disputed. However, performing a gap analysis or reviewing your environmental management situation before you understand where you want to go, or before you have thoroughly considered the implications of an EMS on your business, is not an efficient use of your time or money. There will not be much talk here about the gap analysis; the authors instead prefer to consider the initial review.[1]

The role of the initial review will be discussed later in this chapter. Depending on how well you understand your environmental performance and your company's environmental aspects, you may need to conduct reviews at different steps in the planning and implementation process. Certainly, you need a base level of understanding before you can define environmental aspects and determine impacts, or before you can define your legal and other requirements. However, before you try to determine what existing procedures you have in place or how they can best be utilized in your EMS, the authors believe you need to have already considered several steps in the planning process.

The approach here, therefore, focuses on understanding some basic elements of the EMS process before embarking on a thorough review of your existing operations. Moving along then, the basic steps of the EMS planning process are as follows:

- Developing an environmental policy
- Defining environmental aspects and determining their impacts
- Defining legal and other requirements
- Conducting the initial review
- Setting objectives and targets
- Developing environmental management programs

5.1   The Environmental Policy

Mission statements and business policies are commonly used by companies as part of their external communications. Many, if not most, companies have at one time or another developed a statement which embodies in a brief few sentences what that company's goals and interests are. More often than not these mission statements or business policies are general, optimistic, and altruistic testimonies meant to enhance the image of the company. In the best instances, they form the backbone of the company's operations and provide actual guidance to the company and its employees on how to conduct its business in a way that will meet the long-range goals of the company.

An environmental policy developed for an EMS must be the backbone of the EMS. Any company that has successfully developed an EMS has started with a strong top-management commitment and has made this commitment a part of its business. The environmental policy is a statement of the company's commitment to the environment. As such, it must describe how the company intends to accomplish its environmental goals.

The environmental policy should not be complicated or verbose. Think about what your company wants to accomplish with its EMS. The environmental policy cannot describe the steps to achieving the company's environmental performance goals, but it should provide the framework. When read by employees or external interested parties, it should be clear what the company's EMS is aiming to accomplish.

AMRO was highlighted earlier in this book. AMRO was one of the first companies in the United States to receive ISO 14001 certification. AMRO is

Americas Materials Recovery Operations Environmental Policy

Purpose: This document defines the Americas Materials Recovery Operations policy on protecting the environment.

Scope: This document applies to all of Americas Materials Recovery Operations.

Digital's Americas Materials Recovery Operations (AMRO) has adopted the following general policy:

We will exceed our customer expectations by delivering defect free services with a focus on excellence in the execution of environmentally sound and secure processes. We commit to ensuring the protection of the community and the environment through an environmental management system that recognizes the value of continuous improvement. All site activities are integrated into an environmental management system that commits to compliance to all applicable regulations, corporate and site policies, ISO 14000 standards to improve the environmental aspect of the business.

On the basis of Digital's Earth Vision policy, we recognize that the company is moving into an era of sustainable development, thus we commit to pollution prevention, material recovery and natural resource conservation. Earth Vision provides the foundation for achieving environmental excellence and provides direction for attaining national and global leadership.

AMRO will set goals and measure achievement to address the environmental aspects of the business. These will be reviewed on an annual basis or as business changes dictate.

As a corporation, we seek exemplary solutions to global environmental problems through our operations, products and information technology. As an operation within the corporation, the Americas Materials Recovery Operations organization strives to reclaim and recover the maximum amount of material from electronic products.

This policy, as well as the corporation's Earth vision policy is documented, implemented, maintained and communicated to all employees. It is also posted and available to anyone, upon request.

Fuji Xerox's Basic Environmental Policy

Fuji Xerox recognizes the importance of environmental protection, endeavoring to harmonize corporate activities and environmental protection. From a global point of view, we, Fuji Xerox staff, shall do our best to decrease negative influences on the environment in order to save the valuable natural environment.

1. We shall faithfully observe environmental regulations as we do our best to ensure that none of our operations pose any hazard to environmental health and safety.
2. We shall take every possible measure to save resources and energy through our operations while studying the impact of these operations on the environment.
3. We shall develop and introduce advanced technologies for environmental protection to reduce negative influences on the environment.
4. We shall participate in environmental protection activities to positively promote harmonization with the communities in which we operate.
5. We shall also be responsible for environmental protection in our overseas operations.
6. We shall improve and strengthen our environmental management systems through environmental auditing and other activities.

Fuji Xerox organized the Environmental Safety Promotion Committee and assigned a director to take charge of environmental programs in 1985. In addition, we established a way to incorporate environmental protection measures early in the product planning stage and stepped up recycling activities. Through these in-house organizations and efforts, we work to uphold our basic environmental policy with the aim of realizing the intended results.

a small to medium-sized subsidiary involved in materials reclamation and, although it manufactures nothing, had strong early interest in developing an EMS and seeking ISO 14001 certification. AMRO's environmental policy states simply and clearly that AMRO is committed to the environment and will uphold that commitment through the use of an EMS. The policy goes further to describe actions that AMRO will undertake to fulfill its commitment. These include setting goals, measuring progress, and undertaking annual reviews. Several program areas, such as pollution prevention, materials recovery, and resources conservation, are specified. AMRO's environmental policy makes it clear that AMRO has an EMS in place that includes elements required by ISO 14001, specific environmental management programs in such areas as pollution prevention, materials recovery, and resource conservation. This is how AMRO's environmental policy drives the EMS and how it provides awareness and direction to AMRO employees as to the intent and direction of the EMS.

Fuji Xerox is a much larger company with global operations. Fuji's environmental policy, however, is as simple as AMRO's and accomplishes the same purposes.

Electrolux, another major, global company, requires that every product line manager prepare an action program to ensure that its environmental policy is executed. Electrolux's structure is interesting in that it sets forth seven basic concepts: (1) responsibility, (2) precaution, (3) total approach, (4) preparedness, (5) priorities, (6) market leader, and (7) profitability. This policy makes an important point. Making money is not only okay, but is an integral part of good environmental performance. A financially healthy company has the resources necessary to creating new opportunities for improving environmental performance. This policy illustrates how a company can create awareness of a number of important issues associated with an effective overall environmental management program.

An environmental policy, like all elements of your EMS, can and likely should evolve as you move through the EMS continuous improvement process. Whereas an early policy may need to provide more specific guidance to help educate employees who are mostly unaware of EMS elements, once employees are familiar with EMS and have integrated EMS elements into their operations, the policy plays a different role. The environmental policy

Electrolux Environmental Policy

Responsibility
Our role as a company is to fulfill the needs of society that generate demand for our products. This involves a responsibility for contributing to sustainable development by continuously improving our products and our production processes from an environmental perspective.

Precaution
Precaution must be our guide for all development and production within the Group, in order to avoid irrevocable environmental impact. This requires a cautious approach to activities which might have a serious environmental impact.

Total Approach
We must adopt a total approach in our operations, based on knowledge of every phase of the life cycles of our products, from raw materials and production to use and recycling. We must choose the options that minimize negative environmental impact as well as consumption of raw materials and energy.

Preparedness
Our business development must include an active commitment to development and marketing of products with the least possible environmental impact. As we continuously acquire more knowledge and promote our environmental efforts, we will also be prepared to meet future environmental needs.

Priorities
Our development will involve continuous gradual reduction of the environmental impact of our operations. Our work must be goal-oriented and cost-effective. We will assign priority to our environmental investments on the basis of what is most appropriate in terms of ecology.

Market Leader

Active, far-sighted research and development will enable us to continuously offer products that meet high environmental expectations. An active commitment to the environment, which integrates care for the environment in all our operations and involves a contribution from all our employees, will keep us competitive and will strengthen our position as market leader.

Profitability

Effective use of resources will be a decisive criterion for profitability. Good profitability is a prerequisite for our environmental activities, as it generates resources for investment and development.

Every product line manager is responsible for preparing an action program to ensure that the above policy is carried out. The Electrolux Environmental Affairs Committee is responsible for development and interpretation of this policy and for monitoring its implementation.

---

then needs to reflect the goals of the EMS, maintain awareness, provide ongoing directions, and describe the company's commitment to environmental performance to external interested parties.

The evolution of environmental polices at Baxter illustrates these important considerations. Baxter International is a global medical-products company.

Baxter developed an environmental policy in 1991 with the aim of implementing a state-of-the-art environmental management program within the corporation. This initial policy was very specific in terms of actions to be taken, including unit manager's responsibilities:

1. Environmental Review Board. An Environmental Review Board (ERB) appointed by the Public Policy Committee of the Board of Directors of Baxter is responsible for overseeing implementation of environmental policy. The ERB will review and decide matters of environmental importance and will make an annual report to the Board of Directors.

2. Legal Compliance.   Baxter will comply with all applicable environmental laws.
3. Risk Control.   Baxter will not create unacceptable risks to the environment and will minimize risk to the company from previous, existing and potential environmental conditions.
4. Waste Minimization.   Baxter will aggressively pursue opportunities to minimize the quantity and degree of hazard of the waste that results from its operations. It will reduce toxic and chlorofluorocarbon air emissions 60 percent by 1992 and 80 percent by 1996, from 1988 levels based on equivalent production.
5. Environmental Leadership.   Baxter will work to become a leader in respect for the environment. It will establish and maintain an environmental program to be considered state of art among the Fortune 500 companies. Baxter will accomplish this goal by 1993 in the United States, Puerto Rico and Canada, and by 1996 worldwide.
6. Environmental Coordinators and Managers.   The Manager of each manufacturing and distribution facility, and other division and group managers where appropriate, will appoint a qualified environmental representative to coordinate and manage the unit's environmental program. However, compliance with this Policy is not just the responsibility of these representatives; it is the responsibility of every employee and particularly every manager.
7. Training and Audit.   Corporate environmental personnel, divisions and facilities will provide coordinated, effective environmental training, awareness and audit programs as appropriate.
8. Unit Manager Responsibility.   The manager of each unit of the company will assure that the following are accomplished by the unit wherever relevant:
   8-1. Determine the facts regarding generation and release of pollutants from its facilities and responsibly manage its affairs to minimize any adverse environmental impact.
   8-2. Develop and implement its own environmental management program to comply with this Policy.
   8-3. Select, design, build and operate products, processes and facilities in order to minimize the generation and discharge of waste and other adverse impacts on the environment.

8-4. Utilize control and recycling technology wherever scientifically and economically feasible to minimize the adverse impact on the environment.

The initial policy was revised in 1996 and again in 1997. The primary change in 1997 was the incorporation of health and safety with environmental concerns. Comparing the 1996 revision to the 1991 policy, we see a simpler, more general statement of intent, while maintaining the key goals and action items. Clearly, Baxter's EMS has matured to a point where it is not necessary to have as specific a policy as that needed in 1991. The awareness and direction can be maintained with a policy that reflects the ongoing activities within the EMS.

Baxter's Environmental Policy—Adopted March 17, 1996

Baxter will be a global leader in respecting the environment. Environmental excellence is vital to Baxter's business interests and is consistent with our mission and shared values. Specifically, we commit to the following:

Sustainable Development
We will strive to conserve natural resources and minimize or eliminate adverse environmental effects and risks associated with our products, services and operations.

Compliance
We will meet or exceed all government regulations and comply with all Baxter environmental requirements, including the company's own state-of-the-art environmental-management standards.

Customers
We will work with our customers to help them address their environmental needs.

Employees
We will assure that employees have the awareness, skills and knowledge to carry out this policy.

Suppliers and Contractors
We will work with our suppliers and contractors to enhance environmental performance.

Community and Government
We will participate in community and government environmental initiatives.

Business Integration
We will integrate environmental considerations into our business.

Baxter commits to continuous improvement in environmental performance. We will set goals, measure progress and communicate results. Compliance with this policy is the responsibility of every employee.

5.2 Environmental Aspects, Environmental Impacts, and the Issue of Significance

An environmental aspect is any element of your company's activities, products, or services that can interact upon the environment. The tendency in the United States and other highly regulated societies is to look first at what regulations require in the way of compliance. This misses the point entirely. The importance of the notion of environmental aspects is that it looks at the activities of your company, not at how your company reacts to regulations. The major cultural change that is inherent in the development of an EMS is getting away from a focus on environmental regulations and refocusing on your company's activities and their impact on the environment.

Once you have created a list of environmental aspects, you will likely have identified several that are regulated in one form or another. Your EMS will need to take these regulations into account in dealing with those environmental aspects. However, this is very different from defining an environmental aspect by just looking at regulations. For example, consider only your activities and ignore for the moment any environmental regulations. You may have the following environmental aspects:

- Air emissions
- Energy consumption
- Solid waste disposal
- Resource consumption

These are all environmental aspects of your activities. Some may be regulated—air emissions may or may not be regulated, depending upon the levels and your location; solid waste disposal is likely to be regulated at some level. Nonetheless, each is an environmental aspect whether regulated or not. Regulations will enter into your EMS as part of your environmental programs for addressing these environmental aspects. If regulated, the environmental programs addressing an environmental aspect will need to consider and address those regulations.

Service organizations also have environmental aspects. For example, the U.S. Postal Service identified environmental aspects associated with its vehicles, with the chemicals used to maintain equipment, with solid wastes that are generated, and with the stamps that it sells. Likewise, every company should also consider its services and products when identifying environmental aspects. Consider use and disposal of your products as they relate to interaction with the environment. If you ship your own products or provide service on products, you need to consider the environmental aspects associated with those services. Other considerations include fuel consumption, products used in carrying out the service, or disposal of defective parts. One of the key considerations for AMRO was the degree to which it could recycle or resell components of computer equipment and avoid or decrease the amount of waste disposal.

ISO 14001/14004 recognize that environmental aspects may not be within your ability to control or influence. Therefore, ISO 14001 requires that an organization define only those environmental aspects that it can control or influence. In developing your environmental aspects, regardless of whether your EMS will ultimately need to comply with ISO 14001, you also should consider those that you can control or influence. Your EMS will be designed to meet the goals of your environmental policy; therefore, you do not want to spend time agonizing over environmental aspects of your activities that you cannot control.

For example, you have control over your use of energy, and energy consumption is an environmental aspect of your activities. However, you often cannot control the source of that energy. If the electricity you buy is generated using fossil fuels, then depletion of fossil fuels, air emissions–related issues, and global warming may all be environmental aspects of that electricity generation. They are not, however, environmental aspects over which you have control or influence. Note, however, that if alternate sources of generated electricity were to become available (e.g., through energy deregulation and competitive bargaining), then you might wish to consider electricity generation as an environmental aspect that you could control.

Environmental aspects have associated impacts that may be beneficial or detrimental to the environment. It is these environmental impacts that the EMS will target. A matrix of environmental aspects with associated environmental impacts provides a good way to understand the linkages between aspects and impacts and to ensure that all appropriate impacts are considered. Consider Table 5.1.

An EMS generally cannot, however, tackle every environmental impact your company may identify. Therefore, you need to prioritize the environ-

TABLE 5.1. Environmental Aspects and Some Possible Corresponding Environmental Impacts

Activity/product/service	Environmental aspect	Environmental impact
Heat coating operation (activity)	Energy usage	Natural resource depletion
	Air emissions	Toxicity of contaminants in air
	Raw material usage	Natural resource depletion
Process design engineering (product)	Raw material selection	Natural resource depletion Reduced toxicity of wastes
	Reuse of process residuals	Conservation of resources
HVAC maintenance (service)	Exhaust emissions	Reduction in air emissions
	Energy usage	Reduction in energy usage Conservation of resources

mental impacts and address first those which are most significant. The significance of each identified environmental impact must be considered within the specific framework of your facility. What is significant to another company may not be significant to you. Therefore, you should consider both environmental concerns and business concerns. It can be helpful to quantify elements when possible. In developing your environmental impacts and evaluating their significance, you want to consider the following:

- Whether your facility is located in an environmentally sensitive area or the area requires some other special environmental consideration
- Whether a process failure could result in a more significant or severe environmental impact
- The probability of the environmental impact occurring
- Ecological effects or human health impacts
- The scope of the environmental impacts (local, regional, or global)
- The severity and frequency of any environmental impacts
- How process or product changes or additions would affect the environmental impacts
- Procedures your company has for evaluating the environmental impacts of new projects
- The potential for regulatory and legal liability
- The interest or concerns of interested parties (employees, shareholders, neighbors, and local environmental groups)
- The degree of difficulty associated with changing the impact
- The estimated cost of changing the impact
- How changing an impact may affect other aspects of your operations
- How the environmental impact affects your company's reputation or public image
- The company's environmental policy

The goals should be to address those impacts which most directly affect the environment, those which provide the most immediate environmental performance gain, those which can most easily be mitigated, and those which will result in greatest overall environmental improvement (including resource and energy use issues). Numerous matrices have been reported for use in prioritizing impacts. One good example is the matrix used by AMRO to rank the environmental impacts of its activities (Table 5.2).

TABLE 5.2. Example Environmental Aspects Matrix
Americas Materials Recovery Operations Facilities Weighting Matrix—
Environmental Aspects with Significant Impacts

Department	Activity/ Product/ Service	Environ-mental Aspect	Aspect is actual or potential	Media Affected	Qualify/ quantify/ impacts	Scale of impact	Severity of impact
Facilities	IPV Maint-enance	Potential for accidental chemical spillage	P	Soil/ water	0–10 gal. spill resulting in water/soil contamination	1	1
Facilities	Diesel/ gasoline vehicle maintenance	Exhaust emissions	A	Air	Minimal emissions	1	1
Facilities	Fire suppression system/ maintenance	Potential for CFC air emissions	P	Air	0–210 lbs Halon 1301 discharged to air	1	1
Facilities	Diesel fuel storage	Potential for accidental spillage	P	Water/ soil	0–935 gal diesel fuel spill resulting in water/soil contamination		2
Facilities	Propane distribution system	Gas leaks	P	Air/ property	3,000 ft of pipe	1	1
Facilities	Propane fuel storage	Potential for fire/ explosion	P	Air/ property	30,000 gal	1	4

Environmental concerns

1 = Low   Operational problem, no permanent environment harm, no significant financial loss, no reporting requirement
2 = Medium   Minor regulatory violation, small scale remediation, significant financial loss, reporting required
3 = High   Major regulatory violation, large scale remediation, significant financial loss, reporting required
4 = Catastrophic Imminent threat to human health or the environment, business disruption, major media coverage

As can be seen, AMRO considered both environmental and business concerns using a simple 1 to 4 ranking. NSF International, in its implementation guide for small businesses, provides a similar matrix designed to consider the degree of impact and the frequency of impact for a series of categories (e.g., human health, environment, and resource use), as related to different

Environmental concerns		Business concerns					
Probability of occurrence	Duration of impact	Regulation legal exposure	Difficulty of changing impact	Cost of changing impact	Effect of change on other activities	Concerns of interested parties	Effect on public image
2	1	N/A	N/A	N/A	N/A	N/A	N/A
1	1	N/A	N/A	N/A	N/A	N/A	N/A
1	1	N/A	N/A	N/A	N/A	N/A	N/A
1	2	2	N/A	N/A	N/A	1	1
1	1	1	1	2	1	1	1
1	4	4	N/A	N/A	N/A	4	4

functions of the business (e.g., preproduction, manufacturing, and use and service).

Identifying environmental aspects for your EMS is then a four-part process: (1) develop a list of environmental aspects, (2) screen out those over which you legitimately have no control or influence, (3) identify the environmental impacts for each aspect, and (4) determine the significant impacts. The complexity and magnitude of your list of environmental aspects will depend upon the complexity of your activities. AMRO is a fairly environmentally clean operation and, therefore, had only a few environmental aspects to consider. Larger manufacturing facilities often have countless environmental aspects to consider. Identifying environmental aspects and impacts can sometimes be a major undertaking. Hewlett-Packard, in designing its approach to EMS, reports having started with a commitment through four basic functional areas: (1) design, (2) manufacturing, (3) reuse or recycling, and (4) packaging. For each functional area, they looked at ways to improve environmental performance. For example, for design they considered the environmental attributes of products (e.g., improved energy efficiency, increased use of recycled materials, and preventing or minimizing environmental impacts). For manufacturing, they considered managing chemical use, minimizing hazardous waste generation, or diverting solid waste through reduction, reuse, or recycling. For packaging, they considered creative ways to reduce packaging, the reuse of packaging in delivery, and the increased use of recycled or recyclable materials for packaging. For reuse and recycling, they considered methods for refurbishing and recycling products and designing products to be more easily recyclable.

Involving plant operational personnel is critical. These are the people who know best the aspects of their activities. They may not have considered those aspects directly in terms of the environment, but they certainly know what they do. As discussed early in this section, employee buy-in is critical to the EMS and no more so than at this stage. Use questionnaires or interviews to obtain the information you need about each activity. Environmental compliance audit reports are often a good source of information on your operations, at least for those environmental aspects that have regulations associated with them. When possible, and especially in the United States, look at information already on hand for compliance with state and federal regulations. Things such as types of permits, reporting requirements, and notices of deficiencies can help identify many regulation-related aspects of your operations. Reviewing environmental audit reports also helps to identify areas of your operations where problems have occurred or potentially could. Material safety data sheets (MSDS) or other raw material information can help identify the relative environmental hazards associated with materials at use in your company.

SSI Technologies Inc., at its antilock brake division, used a cross section of employees, including personnel from maintenance, production lines, accounting, and the secretarial pool, to help in defining the environmental aspects. Using four-person teams, SSI challenged each team to identify aspects related to the facility, the community, the state, and the world. The facility was divided into four functionally based categories: (1) raw material transportation, (2) process, (3) disposal, and (4) process waste recycling. Based on feedback from the employees, SSI listed media for possible aspect identification: energy, resources, air, water, soil, noise, human beings, climate, and ecology. SSI's approach raised a key consideration that is important for any company to appraise, which is the notion of not looking only at impacts outside of the plant. The human factor cannot be overlooked. Employees use chemicals for manufacturing or other plant operations; therefore, there are environmental aspects associated with those employees. SSI used a ranking system similar to those described previously to provide a numerical ranking relative to risk frequency and severity.

Ford Canada's aspect identification process was multitiered, starting with a global methodology that set a framework for plants in all countries to complete the process consistent with the Ford Motor Company's business plan. Environmental policies existed at the corporate, country, and facility or site level. These, too, had to be considered in developing environmental aspects for a particular facility in a particular country. Ford Canada had to be cognizant of the corporate and the Canadian environmental policies, as well as those for each facility within Canada. It took a few tries at different facilities before the process began to smooth out. Ford Canada also found it useful to use the services of people from other plants within the global Ford family where formal EMS plans had already been implemented.

Process flow sheets can also help you visualize each step of your activities and spot environmental aspects that are not obvious or intuitive. A process flow approach should include all of the inputs and outputs of each operation or activity. Warner-Lambert Company reports having used process flow sheets it developed to identify and visualize each waste stream coming from its operations, including costs of each to the company. In its appraisal it also examined product packaging and product waste disposal. Costs, as previously noted, are one consideration when prioritizing your environmental impacts. Collecting information on costs as part of the development of environmental aspects and impacts is a smart and efficient approach to ensuring that all relevant information is available for the appraisal of impacts.

Warner Lambert and its consultant, EnSafe, developed an aspect analysis procedure that considered the following:

- Site operations and the preparation of a list of categories for activities, products, and services
- Input from appropriate personnel, through interviews
- Migration and transport pathways and environmental receptors, identified by a site reconnaissance
- Documented environmental policies and related documents

The results were compiled in a series of tables that presented the facilities' environmental aspects and associated impacts, organized by activity, product, or service.

The end result of the environmental aspects identification process is a list of significant environmental impacts that your company's EMS will address. The importance of this step in the EMS development process cannot be overemphasized. Everything else in your EMS will flow from the selection of significant environmental impacts that reflect the environmental performance goals set out in your company's environmental policy.

5.3   Identifying Legal and Other Requirements

The identification and evaluation of environmental aspects requires an understanding of your company's legal and other requirements. ISO 14001 also requires that your company "establish and maintain a procedure to identify and have access to legal and other requirements" that are applicable to your company. Implicit in this requirement is the ability to identify and track new or developing requirements. Many companies have procedures in place to track applicable regulations, especially in the United States. Other requirements are generally not tracked in as formal a way, but will need to be for ISO 14001. Identification of legal and other requirements should be part of any EMS, even if ISO 14001 certification is not desired.

There are basically three reasons to consider nonregulatory performance criteria: they are a de facto regulation because they are the standard of care for the type of activities you are involved in; it is politically expedient to consider them because they will impact your standing in your community or your ability to market your product (local agreements with neighbors, interest groups, and so forth); or they provide assurance of environmental performance in areas not covered by regulatory requirements. All of these will have some impact on the effectiveness of your EMS. Areas not covered by regulatory requirements, but important to your effective management of your environmental performance, might include the following:

- Employee roles and responsibilities
- Training and awareness
- Process design engineering
- Product stewardship
- Energy conservation and management
- Pollution prevention and natural resource conservation

Legal requirements include any regulatory or statutory requirements that apply to the environmental aspects of your company. Other requirements can be a variety of nonregulatory performance criteria, whether from sources outside your company or developed by your company for internal use. Other requirements could include the following:

- Industry codes of practice (e.g., CMA Responsible Care or API STEP)
- Criteria recommended by association groups to which your company belongs
- Governmental nonregulatory guidances
- Agreements with local authorities, neighbors, or public interest groups
- Global initiatives (e.g., ICC Charter for Sustainable Development)
- Customer product standards
- Internal standard operating procedures
- Corporatewide operating criteria

Your EMS should have procedures for tracking applicable legal and other requirements, identifying changes, and updating procedures to reflect changes. Most companies that the authors have interviewed have relied upon existing procedures developed for tracking regulatory compliance requirements. In some cases, these procedures needed to be expanded to address nonregulatory requirements.

As you move through the EMS continual improvement cycle, changes to regulations or newly emerging legal and other requirements will need to be considered in the review of your EMS and in the evaluation and modification of environmental aspects or objectives and targets. The environmental policies highlighted earlier in Section 5.1 each specifically address legal and other requirements, both internal and external to companies.

There are many sources that your company may find helpful in identifying and tracking legal requirements. You will likely want to use multiple sources, since any one source may not provide complete coverage of your operations. Some possible sources include the following:

- Notifications or guidance from governmental environmental regulatory agencies
- Business or industry groups to which you may belong
- Seminars or training courses (several commercial courses are available)
- Internet web pages (e.g., epa.gov for U.S. EPA guidance; clay.net for state and federal links)
- Commercially available regulatory tracking services or databases
- Environmental consultants.

The best approach is the use of in-house procedures supported by a mix of outside help. No single outside source is likely to provide a complete enough program. To comply with ISO 14001 you will need to demonstrate that you have a system in place to keep you current on legal requirements. Your company should develop that system specific to your needs and use whatever mix of sources will reasonably provide the information needed, remaining aware of the limitations of any specific source.

Governmental notifications tend to be complicated and difficult to understand, especially in terms of the practical applicability to your company. Not all levels of government provide such notifications in an organized or dependable manner. Industry groups usually provide good updates or seminars on the hot regulatory issues, but they cannot address every new regulation. They may be a good source for trends in developing regulations. They are also a good source for networking with other companies similar to yours and for exchanging ideas on what types of tracking systems have provided good results. Commercial sources vary considerably in quality and coverage. Those that are good usually provide good coverage with frequent updates at the federal level, but provide less coverage as you move down through the levels of government. Depending on the total coverage you need and the frequency of updates, the cost can be high. Professional environmental consultants are a useful source for understanding the applicability of new regulations or for assistance in tracking developing regulations. However, few consultants are knowledgeable enough in more than a few areas of environmental regulations to provide in-depth tracking information. Therefore, you need a team of consultants covering several disciplines to achieve adequate coverage.

5.4   The Role of the Initial Review

The initial environmental review determines a company's current position in terms of its interaction with the environment. This initial determination will provide important data needed to begin the planning phase of ISO 14001 implementation. Your initial environmental review should provide a snapshot of the current state of your business relative to the environment. The review could consider such areas of your business as the following:

- The regulatory and legislative requirements determined to be applicable to your business
- The environmental aspects defined for your business
- How you track or apply industry standards, codes of practice, regulations, internal company requirements, or similar guidelines and criteria
- What environmental management practices you already have in place, including procedures or programs
- What activities or internal processes exist that could enable or impede your ability to achieve better environmental performance

You may also want to consider the views of parties outside your company who may have an interest in your environmental performance. These parties could include shareholders, financial backers, neighbors, local interest groups, environmental activist groups, or local governmental entities (e.g., boards and commissions).

Management should first decide what areas of your business or what outside parties you plan to review. You should also define the scope of the review: Will it be companywide, or within a single business unit, a single site, or a specific operation? Having decided what you need to review, there are several techniques that could be useful, depending upon the nature of the information you are trying to collect. Companies have considered the following methods:

- Using focused questionnaires, which provide responses that are as unambiguous as possible
- Reviewing existing company records, procedures, and so forth
- Performing site inspections
- Reviewing audit results
- Interviewing company personnel or outside parties
- Developing checklists
- Reviewing practices within the company that have successfully provided environmental improvement
- Reviewing procedures or practices of other similar organizations that have demonstrated environmental improvement

Volvo Cars Europe Industry (VCEI) defined the initial review as a comprehensive analysis of environmental issues, environmental impacts, and environmental performance. VCEI defined 12 issues to be covered (e.g., energy, waste, noise, etc.) and followed basic environmental auditing requirements. VCEI performed its initial review after the adoption of its environmental policy, but before it began the introduction of environmental management programs. The initial review required three days and was performed by a corporate environmental auditor and two other persons involved in the EMS implementation. The audit activities included a general plant tour, visits to specific areas, and interviews with key persons and with management. An audit report provided the review information for the EMS implementation process. VCEI chose this process for its initial review because it had an experienced environmental audit team and processes in place and, therefore, could perform the initial review at a low cost.

Numerous checklists and questionnaires have been developed by companies and consultants alike for the purpose of developing initial review information. SCIMED Life Systems, Inc. developed a self-assessment tool that is easy to use and understand, provides information that could be used to determine compliance with ISO 14001, provides measurable results, eliminates smoking guns, and can be completed in two days. The tool consists of 170 questions linked to the requirements of ISO 14001. There are five responses per question, each response designed to provide clearly defined responses. There is a guidance section for each question, and the entire tool runs in a Window-based computer application. A question related to environmental aspects, for example, would be identified by an ISO section (ISO Section 4.3.1) and an EHS category (EHS Category: EHS Management Systems). SCIMED identified the following EHS categories for consideration:

- EHS management systems
- Hazardous substances management
- Health and safety
- Air and water quality
- Hazardous materials transportation
- Pollution prevention
- Waste management
- Emergency response.

The SCIMED assessment process involves selecting a facility-specific team composed of operations, R&D, quality, EHS, human resources, finance, and sales or marketing. This team reviews each question in a roundtable forum to develop a consensus response. A facilitator is used to record responses and interpret questions when necessary. A predetermined goal for each question is compared to the site-specific score, and a report is generated that lists those questions where the goal was higher than the actual score. The facility-specific management team then prioritizes the list, assigns responsibilities, and defines time frames for completion. SCIMED has found that the self-assessment tool provides for a consensus decision, which enhances buy-in, and that the discussion of issues has educational side benefits. The scoring process also provides a visible measurement for determining outcomes.

The process designed by SCIMED is very useful in multiple-facility settings, but is likely to be too complex for the smaller business. However, concepts used in the self-assessment tool can be applied in a less intensive manner for the smaller business. Likewise, there are numerous sources of information available that can be useful to any company, including the following:

- Regulatory agencies, for help in determining the existence and applicability of regulations
- Other companies in your industry or industry group, to exchange information or determine industry standards
- Libraries, databases, or online services, including Internet web pages or technical discussion groups
- Associations to which your customers belong
- Manufacturers of the equipment used by your company
- Contractors your firm employs (e.g., waste haulers, disposal facilities, and hazardous waste cleanup firms)
- Environmental management consultants

The results and findings, as well as the process used for the initial review (e.g., information sources and techniques employed) should be documented. The information developed should be summarized in a manner that will allow management to understand the current state of your organization relative to environmental performance. This should allow management to identify areas where environmental performance needs to be improved and to identify opportunities that could lead to better or more efficient environmental performance.

5.5   Defining Objectives and Targets

An *objective* is established to provide specific emphasis and direction to meet your company's environmental policy. The *target* is a specific and measurable end point, related to an objective, which can demonstrate achievement or progress toward achievement of the objective. Reduction of air emissions is an objective. A reduction of 15 percent over the next 6 months is a target. Increased environmental awareness among employees is an objective. Completion of training for 50 percent of your employees within 1 year and 100 percent of your employees within 2 years is a target. Redesign of a product line to decrease raw material consumption is an objective. A 25-percent increase in the ratio of recycled materials to raw materials within 1 year is a target.

The objectives and targets must reflect the environmental policy set by top management. They should also take into account the identified significant environmental aspects, legal and other requirements (including financial, operational, and business requirements), and the technological options for meeting targets. Objectives and targets can be developed for specific processes, facilities, or business units, or they can be developed to apply to an entire corporation. Therefore, the development of objectives and targets will first depend upon their scope of application.

Management at the appropriate level for the specific objectives and targets should be involved in the development process. Likewise, employees who will have the ultimate responsibility for achieving the objectives and targets should have input into their development. Your implementation team should work closely with the appropriate managers and employees to ensure that objectives and targets are developed in a manner consistent with the environmental policy and the identified significant environmental aspects.

The objectives flow from the environmental aspects and provide the specific goals that management has selected to address the environmental aspects. Expanding on the examples provided earlier for environmental aspects, the corresponding objectives might be as seen in Table 5.3.

Objectives will change over time, as your EMS goes through each continual improvement cycle. The objectives and targets are developed to address the significant environmental aspects, not every environmental aspect identified. Therefore, the process of prioritizing environmental aspects and selecting objectives to address them is ongoing. Objectives will be met and become obsolete. Likewise, as the significant environmental aspects are redefined based on EMS review cycles, the objectives and targets will also be reviewed and amended, and new objectives will be selected.

A key feature of the EMS is the ability to track the progress toward achieving an objective and its target as a means of measuring the performance of the EMS. Therefore, specific measurable indicators should be established for each target. Consequently, the selection of targets must consider the ability to measure progress toward achieving the target.

Progress toward achieving targets can be measured using environmental performance indicators. The selection and use of environmental performance

TABLE 5.3. Environmental Aspects, Impacts, and Some Possible Corresponding Objectives

Activity/product/ service	Environmental aspect	Environmental impact	Objective
Heat coating operation (activity)	Energy usage	Natural resource depletion	Reduction in energy usage
	Air emissions	Toxicity of air contaminants	Reduction in air emissions
	Raw material usage	Natural resource depletion	Increased recycling/reuse
Process design engineering (product)	Raw material selection	Natural resource depletion	Design for recyclable inputs
		Reduced toxicity of wastes	Design for "cleaner" raw materials
	Reuse of process residuals	Conservation of resources	Design for reuse of process outputs
HVAC maintenance (service)	Exhaust emissions	Reduction in air emissions	Maintain for efficient combustion
	Energy usage	Reduction in energy usage	Maintain for maximum efficiency
		Conservation of resources	

indicators is discussed in Chapter 7. Likewise, a guidance standard on environmental performance evaluation is being developed by ISO (ISO 14031). Environmental performance indicators need to be developed by your company to measure environmental performance in specific areas. Unlike audits, which provide a point-in-time appraisal of your compliance with specific requirements, environmental performance indicators should provide a measurement over time to show trends toward improved performance or achieving an objective.

5.6 Developing Environmental Management Programs

The environmental management programs are the mechanism by which the actions identified by the implementation team during planning are actually carried out. Whereas the implementation plan may set a milestone for some portion of your EMS planning or implementation to be completed, it is the environmental management programs that will ensure that the appropriate people and resources undertake the appropriate tasks to meet that milestone.

The environmental management programs should be developed for discrete tasks or activities and should designate a person responsible for achieving the objectives and targets associated with those tasks or activities. Likewise, they should describe the available resources committed to completing these tasks or activities. Finally, they should set a time by which it is expected that the program(s) will be in place. 3M Corporation's Dental Products facility developed a traditional GANTT chart (named for its developer) to aid in the implementation of its environmental programs. The GANTT chart was based on the results of self-assessment. The benefit of the GANTT chart approach is that it ensures that activities occur in a logical sequence and that events have not been planned which rely upon other activities not yet completed.

The environmental management programs are a natural result of the planning activities completed by the implementation team. Therefore, the implementation team plays a key role in identifying the necessary programs. However, throughout the planning process, managers and employees should have had inputs into the process (e.g., in developing objectives and targets). Therefore, the development of action-specific environmental management programs should include managers and employees in the areas in which each program will focus.

NIBCO Incorporated, a worldwide manufacturer of plumbing products, developed its EMS around two discrete but associated concepts: Total Quality Environmental Management and Waste Minimization and Pollution Prevention (WM/PP). NIBCO expanded on its ISO 9002 QMS by applying the same concepts to environmental management, integrating control, monitoring, and other management features of QMS with the cost savings and other benefits of WM/PP. Likewise, 3M Dental Products relied significantly on its ISO 9001 experience. Of 22 documented EMS procedures, 8 came directly from 3M's ISO 9001 Quality Manual (training, management system documentation, document control, monitoring and measurement, nonconformance, records, management system auditing, and management review).

Like everything before them, the development of environmental management programs starts with the specific environmental policy commitment. For each commitment there is an identified set of targets and objectives (there may be only one objective and target, but usually there are more). Generally, an environmental management program will be needed for each objective and target. Finally, each environmental management program should have its list of action items. Table 5.4 provides a simple example of the development process for the environmental management programs for one environmental policy commitment.

Two companies that have used somewhat unique approaches to implementing environmental programs are Acushnet Rubber and Wilton Armetale.

TABLE 5.4. Development of an Environmental Policy Commitment

Policy commitment	Objective	Target	Environmental programs	Action items
Reduce hazardous emissions	Reduce air emissions from coatings operations	15% less VOC emissions in 9 months	VOC coatings reduction	Install VOC controls Switch to low-VOC coatings
	Maintain efficient HVAC combustion	25% reduction in HVAC malfunctions	HVAC maintenance	Maintain daily log Train maintenance personnel
	Design for "cleaner" raw materials	Reduce use of hazardous raw materials by 30%	Process design	Awareness training for design engineers "Clean design" awards

Acushnet Rubber Company, Inc. made strong use of its existing toxics use reduction (TUR) plan. The TUR was developed as part of a Massachusetts state program and employed parts of the tracking system required by ISO 14001. Acushnet had already examined its manufacturing processes in preparation for its TUR, and this information was extremely useful in developing appropriate EMS programs. Wilton Armetale is a Pennsylvania foundry whose approach was to develop partnerships with an environmental consultant and with the Pennsylvania Department of Environmental Protection (PA-DEP). While some companies may view a partnership with a state agency as a bold, if not dangerous, move, Wilton has found the process beneficial. Wilton, with inputs from both partners, enhanced existing environmental policies while looking at all aspects of pollution prevention. The partnerships have led to the development of ISO 14001 guidelines that can be used throughout the industry. The partnerships have generally provided Wilton with valuable inputs to its EMS process.

CHAPTER 6

IMPLEMENTING YOUR COMPANY'S EMS

If you have reached the implementation phase, your top management has committed to the concepts of EMS and has developed a clear environmental policy and objectives and targets. The most important step is to begin to focus your people and available resources toward the strategy and structure of your EMS. You may choose to implement the EMS in stages to lessen the cultural and financial impact. How you implement your EMS will depend on such factors as the level of awareness of environmental requirements, expected benefits, and available resources.

There are six basic components that you should address when implementing your EMS. These are:

1. Establishing a structure and responsibilities
2. Providing training and ensuring awareness and competence
3. Establishing internal and external communication
4. Documenting the EMS and providing document control
5. Ensuring operational control
6. Establishing emergency preparedness and response

6.1 Defining EMS Structure and Responsibility and Ensuring Resources

The structure of your EMS depends on the size and organization of your company and the degree to which you have existing management processes in place. How you set responsibilities for implementing and maintaining your EMS is based on the personnel resources available. Elements of your EMS should be integrated into the mainstream of your other business management functions whenever possible. This not only provides a more efficient overall management approach, but ensures that environmental performance becomes an integral part of your day-to-day business practices.

An EMS is first a management system. Therefore, most elements of the EMS should be capable of being integrated into your business practices. Several EMS implementation elements described in this section should be viewed as extensions of existing business management elements. For example:

- Procedures for allocating resources
- Records and data management
- Employee performance, appraisal, and reward
- Employee job descriptions, training, and growth
- Operational procedures
- Reporting structures and responsibilities

Management must define the resources necessary to carry out its environmental policy, objectives, and targets. Your management may want to consider the benefits of the EMS and balance them against the costs. Typical benefits might include reduced waste costs and reduced regulatory liabilities. Resources should include people, time allocation, finances, technical support, and specialized skills, as necessary. Small and medium-sized companies often have limited resources and much simpler organizational structures, which results in constraints on their ability to implement the many elements of their EMS. To overcome or mitigate these constraints, consider collaborative arrangements, such as the following:

- Participating in organizations that include larger companies with technologies and insights to share
- Teaming with other small companies to develop strategies together, share knowledge or ideas, jointly undertake technological development, or jointly engage and use professional consultants
- Attending EMS training programs
- Making use of nonprofit research facilities or universities for innovative ideas

Top management should appoint a management person, given defined responsibility and authority, to implement and maintain your EMS in a manner consistent with your environmental policy, objectives, and targets. This person should also have responsibility for reporting progress and performance of the EMS to top management for their review. This person may be the leader or a member of the implementation team, but should at the very least be intimately familiar with the implementation process. This person must have clear senior management authority to make things happen without encountering debates on organizational ownership or turf definitions.

Madison Gas & Electric Company took a tiered approach to assigning roles and responsibilities. The Management Environmental Task Force (MET) consists of senior managers and establishes environmental policies, performs strategic planning, and provides resources to the second tier implementation team, the Green Team Leaders (GTL). The GTL is the implementing arm of the MET and has representatives from the operating and services departments, including union representation.

Employee responsibilities should be set by managers at the appropriate level consistent with the roles and responsibilities developed for your EMS. However, everyone in your company should be accountable for participating in and supporting your EMS and be accountable for the company's environmental performance.

Organizations have very different business approaches and organizational structures. Therefore, there is no single approach to assigning responsibilities. You must ensure that each aspect of your EMS has the necessary responsibilities defined and assigned so that it functions as designed. Likewise, employees whose activities will impact each EMS element must be given and must understand specific responsibilities. In small companies, many roles may be fulfilled by the same person. Milan Screw Products is a small manufacturing company with fewer than 50 employees. Milan established a cross-functional environmental task group (ETG) which consists of five representatives from production, support, and management. The participation of shop-floor employees was found by Milan to be critically essential to the success of the EMS. Likewise, participation in the ETG heightened environmental awareness.

The following list provides some examples of roles and responsibilities and the company position responsible, which will vary depending upon your company's approach to implementation (companywide versus segments). As previously mentioned, small companies may have several functions handled by a single individual.

Role and Responsibility	*Typical Person or Position Responsible*
Environmental policy, objectives, and targets	President, unit manager, or plant manager
Tracking legal and other requirements	Environmental manager
Training, awareness, and competence	Senior operations manager and environmental manager
EMS documentation and recordkeeping	Senior operations manager
Communications	Plant manager or operations managers
Emergency preparedness and response	Operations managers and safety manager
Develop and maintain operational procedures	Senior operations manager and operations managers
Compliance with EMS procedures	All employees

6.2 Ensuring Awareness and Competence and Providing Training

Environmental awareness is a central tenet of any effective EMS. It is through awareness at all levels of your organization that real improvement in environmental performance can occur. If all employees are aware of the ways in which your company's operations impact the environment and how their personnel performance can impact the environment, then it is expected that most employees will choose to perform in a manner most beneficial to the environment. As stated in ISO 14001 (Section 4.3.2.4), "[I]t is the commitment of the individual people, in the context of shared environmental values, that transforms an environmental management system from paperwork into an effective process."

Top management must build awareness through training and build motivation through programs aimed at encouraging improved environmental performance and conformance with the EMS. That is, your management must not only develop the environmental policy, objectives, targets, and EMS, but it must be committed to ensuring that the EMS is understood, accepted, and embraced by employees at all levels of your company. Top management must make acceptance of and compliance with the EMS a part of the company's culture and job performance expectations by taking the following actions:

- Recognizing and rewarding good environmental performance or achievement of objectives and targets
- Encouraging employee suggestions and inputs for environmental improvement
- Encouraging and supporting employee environmental performance initiatives
- Including environmental performance into employee performance reviews
- Making environmental performance a factor in management performance reviews, and punishing noncompliance with the EMS

Everyone in your organization has to receive some level of training, depending upon their job function and its potential to impact upon the environmental performance of the company. Employees at all levels and in all functions must understand the following:

- The importance to the environmental performance of your company of complying with the environmental policy and the requirements of your EMS
- The significant environmental impacts of their particular work activities and how their performance can benefit the environment
- Their roles and responsibilities pursuant to the company's EMS and subsequent environmental performance
- The consequences of their failure to perform or their departure from specified operational procedures

Training is a key functional area in QMS, and companies with a QMS in place should not reinvent the wheel. Companies such as NIBCO, 3M Dental Products, and AMRO have taken advantage of existing training cultures within their companies that were developed for their QMS, and have adapted or enhanced them as necessary to meet their EMS training needs.

There are basically three levels of training: awareness training, EMS procedures training, and job-specific-training. Each has a different potential audience and serves a different role in ensuring employee training and awareness.

Awareness training provides your employees with the information necessary to understand how their job activities have an impact on the environment and on the company's environmental performance. It also introduces them to the concepts of an EMS and how your top management's environmental policy, objectives, and targets provide a committed approach to improving your company's environmental performance. It also serves to motivate employees at all levels of the organization to support the EMS.

Anyone in your company who has a defined responsibility in your EMS needs to understand that responsibility and its relationship to the entire EMS process. *EMS procedures training* has the aim of teaching employees about your EMS. All employees could benefit from some level of EMS procedures training, even if it is just a basic overview of the roles and responsibilities. But those employees with defined roles and responsibilities will require detailed training which includes the level of detail necessary for them to carry out their charge (e.g., detailed procedures, forms, reporting requirements, deadlines, etc.).

ISO 14001 requires that employees with job responsibilities that directly interact with the environment have the necessary education and training. This is a reasonable consideration for any EMS, even if certification is not desired. To accomplish this, you need to ensure that these employees, or those employees who begin an environmentally sensitive job, receive *job-specific training* to ensure that they know how to perform the job and are aware of the job activity's potential impact on the environment. For example, an employee operating a solvent degreaser must be trained to operate the degreaser in a manner that has the least impact on environmental performance. Your EMS should document that this employee has had this specific training.

This does not necessarily mean that you have to hold training courses every time a new person is hired or an employee's job function changes. Initially, you may want to hold a training program for a group of employees with similar job activities. But training does not necessarily require classroom training sessions. A supervisor could have responsibility for training employees on a particular piece of environmentally sensitive equipment. This could be done in the plant or on the job, as long as it was documented that the employee knew the required information in advance of beginning work.

Milan Screw understands the difficulty that a small company can have in providing the time necessary to meet EMS training needs. Milan has conducted training sessions half an hour before or after normal shifts, and has used lunchtime brown bag training. In this instance, employees are not taking their lunch break, but are receiving pay while they eat and learn. To deal with the issue of new employees or reassigned employees, Milan has developed videotaped training.

Your training program should consider, in a stepwise fashion, the following training components:

- Identify your employee training needs.
- Develop your training plan to address those specific needs.
- Ensure that your training program is in conformance with applicable regulatory or internal company requirements.
- Select and train targeted employee groups.
- Document the content, targeted group, frequency, and effectiveness of your training program.
- Evaluate and review completed training programs.

Your company's training should be targeted to specific employee groups to ensure the most efficient information transfer. Different groups have different needs and concerns, depending upon either level in the management structure or type of job responsibility. The most efficient transfer of information occurs when the trainees are interested in the subject matter being presented and it has relevance to their own responsibilities. Upper management personnel have different concerns and responsibilities than middle managers or operational-level employees. Likewise, employees with maintenance-type job responsibilities have different concerns and outlooks than employees with operations-related job responsibilities. Therefore, training should be provided to groups of employees with similar jobs or management responsibilities so that the training can be presented in a manner specific to their concerns and the viewpoint of your company.

Wolstenholme International found employee training and employees' commitment to the process the key factors to successfully implementing the company's EMS. The company's targeted training approach involved the following components:

- General briefings, conducted by senior managers, to all line employees
- Focused training to selected individual groups, conducted by the EHS manager
- Regular meetings of the management team to address procedural requirements
- Focused management review training for supervisors
- Comprehensive training in auditing, spill response, and emergency procedures for the implementation team

Some of the best solutions for reducing the company's negative environmental impacts came from shop-floor personnel and supervisors, and were the result of training and briefings combined with the formation of employee task groups.

An EMS should have elements in place to ensure that employees working in environmentally sensitive job activities are competent to conduct the job functions assigned to them. Ensuring employee competence involves basically three steps:

1. Identify environmentally sensitive job activities.
2. Develop minimum education and experience requirements for each identified environmentally sensitive job activity.
3. Ensure that employees in environmentally sensitive job activities meet the minimum education and experience requirements.

Management needs to identify environmentally sensitive job activities in order to determine the appropriate training required and to identify the employees who require particular training. The place to start is to determine the job activities related to your identified environmental aspects. For example, if air emissions is one of your environmental aspects, then some possible job activities would include paint booth operator, solvent degreaser operator, hazardous waste storage technician, or baghouse maintenance foreman. Each of these employees performs a job activity that could impact the environment and, therefore, your company's environmental performance.

Management also needs to develop minimum education and experience requirements for each identified environmentally sensitive job activity. If your company's human resources department has job descriptions for your employees, then you have a good start toward complying with this element. You just need to ensure that job descriptions for the identified environmentally sensitive job activities include specific requirements related to the environmentally sensitive nature of the job. If your company does not have job descriptions, then the task is more detailed. You will need to ensure that the basic requirements for the job are detailed, as well as the specific environmental considerations. For example, a baghouse maintenance foreman needs to have basic skills unrelated to the environmental nature of the job (good machinist, understands equipment, etc.). These skills will need to be described, as well as the specific requirements related to the environment.

Such requirements may be based on education, experience, or a combination of both. They may require only that the employee have received the necessary in-house training to perform the job activity. The goal is to reasonably ensure that the employee is capable of carrying out the job activities required.

After you have completed the first two steps in this process and have identified the jobs and the requirements, you must either ensure that all employees in the identified jobs meet the requirements or put a plan in place to ensure that they will receive the necessary training to comply with the requirements within a set time period. New or reassigned employees who are beginning an environmentally sensitive job activity will need to meet the minimum requirements or receive adequate training prior to assuming the job activity. You should consider contractors' issues during implementation of any EMS. ISO 14001 requires that you ensure that the contractors who work on your site have the knowledge and expertise to perform their duties in a manner which will not impact the environment nor impact your company's environmental performance.

6.3   Communicating EMS Issues

Internal and, if desired, external communication can allow your organization to do the following:

- Demonstrate its commitment to the environment.
- Handle questions or concerns related to your environmental aspects.
- Increase awareness of your company's environmental policy, objectives, targets, and EMS.

- Provide information about your company's EMS and its performance.

Further, internal communication of the results of EMS measurements, audits, or management reviews need to be provided to the people in your company who are responsible for environmental performance. Likewise, providing information to your employees, and to outside interested parties if desired, raises awareness of your EMS efforts, provides motivation, and garners acceptance of your efforts to improve your environmental performance.

In developing communication processes, you could consider the following:

- How to make your company's environmental policy available to the public, if desired
- How to communicate your company's environmental policy and environmental performance to employees, shareholders, or other outside parties, if desired
- How to receive and respond to concerns or suggestions from employees and, if desired, from parties outside your organization
- How to provide measurement and monitoring results, audit results, and other information concerning the performance of your EMS to the appropriate people within your company to ensure continued improvement of your EMS

Communication of EMS and environmental performance information can be related to your employees through the following means:

- Postings on the company bulletin board
- Internal newspapers or magazines
- E-mail messages
- Group picnics, fairs, and so forth
- Regular staff meetings

Communication of EMS and environmental performance information can be related to external parties through the following means:

- The company's annual report
- Regulatory submissions

- Public government records
- Publications of industry associations to which your company belongs
- News releases
- Paid advertisements
- Company open house days
- Company information hotline telephone numbers

Lucent Technologies Microelectronics Group reports that a distinctive element of the company's implementation process has been the interaction with the local community. Company facilities have formed local environmental advisory groups (LEAGs), which meet periodically to discuss such issues as identification of significant environmental aspects and impacts and the associated potential objectives and targets. This process has reportedly resulted in a growing mutual trust, where the community has a better appreciation of the problems that can arise and a greater comfort that problems will be addressed effectively.

Chapter 9 looks in more detail at the whole spectrum of environmental performance reporting.

6.4 EMS Documentation and Document Control

Documentation of your EMS provides a concrete record of your company's environmental objectives and targets, the environmental programs established to implement your EMS, and the roles and responsibilities assigned to implement and maintain your EMS. It aids in building and maintaining employee awareness. It also provides a standard against which your EMS and your environmental performance can be evaluated.

The EMS documentation will vary considerably depending upon the type, size, and complexity (relative to environmental performance) of your organization. If you can integrate your EMS elements into existing business management systems, then the EMS documentation should be integrated into the documentation for the existing business management system. You may also consider developing a summary of your EMS documentation to provide an easily read overview.

In general, the summary should demonstrate that your EMS is appropriate to your company's activities, products, or services. The following items could be included in an EMS documentation summary:

- A statement of your environmental policy
- A listing of your significant environmental aspects
- A listing of your objectives and targets, with a brief explanation of the procedures used to develop them
- A description of the key roles and responsibilities
- A listing of EMS procedures and a map guiding the reader to the location of each procedure
- A description of the integration, if any, of EMS elements and other business management elements

Document control requires that your company develop and maintain procedures that will ensure the following:

- Documents (including procedures, data, or records) can be located.
- Documents are periodically reviewed and revised as appropriate, as necessary to the maintenance of your EMS.
- Documents and revisions are approved by the appropriate personnel.
- The most current versions of documents are available at operational locations where they are needed to perform EMS functions.
- Obsolete documents are promptly removed from use at all locations where they have been previously distributed and, if required to be saved for legal or regulatory purposes, are clearly marked as obsolete.

Document control at some level is important to the functioning of your EMS. Documents and records provide the day-to-day information needed by your employees to perform their responsibilities pursuant to your EMS and to collect and store the information required by the EMS. Document control procedures ensure that the necessary information is available to your employees. Likewise, the document control procedures ensure that the information collected by your employees is available to management (to review EMS performance) or to other employees who need that information to perform their EMS requirements.

Key issues that should be kept in mind in developing EMS documentation procedures include the following:

- Ensuring that documents are useful and are easily understood by the specific user for which the document is intended

- Ensuring that documents are dated when issued and each time they are revised, and that they are retained for a specific time period
- Ensuring that documents are easily identifiable and are organized in a manner that allows them to be associated with the appropriate company, organizational units, functions, activities, or contact persons for which they are intended
- Ensuring that documents are reviewed and revised based on specific criteria (such as design changes, new personnel, new products, and new regulatory requirements), and are approved by the appropriate person prior to issuance or reissuance
- Ensuring that controls are in place to identify and remove from use in a timely manner any obsolete documents

6.5 Developing Operational Procedures

Implementation of your EMS is accomplished by developing and using specific operational procedures for environmentally sensitive job activities, which ensures that employees at all levels of your company perform these job activities in a manner consistent with the company's environmental policy. Successful performance of these specific operational procedures will ensure that the company meets its environmental objectives and targets. This is operational control.

You can ensure that environmentally sensitive activities are controlled by developing operational procedures that have the following characteristics:

- Cover those situations which, absent the specific operational procedures, could result in deviations from your company's environmental policy and prevent meeting your company's environmental objectives and targets.
- Contain detailed and specific operational criteria.
- Relate directly to your company's environmental aspects.
- Can be and are communicated to and provide requirements for suppliers and contractors used by your company.

Operational procedures can be developed by considering three types of activities which could contribute to your company's environmental performance:

1. Activities related to preventing pollution or conserving resources in new capital projects, process redesign, new products, or facility acquisitions or closures
2. Routine daily activities related to the efficient and effective operations of your company
3. Strategic planning activities to anticipate and respond to changing environmental requirements

Some examples of activities related to preventing pollution or conserving resources in new capital projects, process redesign, new products, or facility acquisitions or closures might include the following:

- Process design engineering
- Research and development into new products or processes
- Purchasing of new raw materials
- Negotiating and contracting for property acquisition

Some examples of routine daily activities related to the efficient and effective operations of your company might include the following:

- Waste handling and storage
- Building and equipment maintenance
- Laboratories
- Waste stream treatment.

Some examples of strategic planning activities to anticipate and respond to changing environmental requirements might include the following:

- Product green labeling
- Elimination of wastes for landfilling
- Elimination of fugitive emissions

New England Power's Brayton Point generating facility has developed hundreds of *green* operating procedures which address the environmental aspects of their various operations. The utility company's consultant, QST Environmental Inc., begins by interviewing the personnel responsible for performing a particular operation. Where written procedures already exist, they form the basis for the new green procedure. Based on the interviews and the written procedure, when available, QST identifies both environmental and safety issues associated with each step of the operation. Based on the issues identified, appropriate actions, precautions, notifications, and so forth are incorporated into the procedure to ensure that legal and other requirements are satisfied. Although Brayton Point has not developed a formal EMS at this time, the green procedures form a strong foundation for the operational control that will be needed as part of an EMS. The process for developing green procedures just described is an excellent example of how a company can adapt or formalize existing procedures to meet the needs of an EMS.

6.6 Emergency Preparedness and Response

Your EMS should ensure that your company develops and maintains adequate procedures to identify whether a potential exists for accidents and emergency situations (including from abnormal operating conditions), define how you would respond to accidents and emergency situations, and define how you would mitigate any environmental impact that might result from such accidents or emergencies. You must review and revise, if needed, these procedures after any actual accident or emergency. Finally, you must also periodically test such procedures, whenever practicable. In the United States, most companies already are required to have an emergency response plan in place if they handle hazardous materials. If your company has such a plan, then you should determine if it meets the requirements of your EMS; you may need go no further. It is likely that most emergency response plans developed and documented for compliance with U.S. regulations will be sufficient.

An emergency response plan could include the following components:

- A description of the emergency response responsibilities—personnel, their roles, their responsibilities, and notification requirements
- A description of the available emergency response resources, including fire, police, spill containment services, and so forth
- Details on the need for and proper procedures for communication regarding the situation, including, as appropriate, contacting regulatory agencies, local officials, the press, key management personnel, and so forth

- A description of the specific types of actions to be taken for various types of emergency situations (e.g., fires, spills, and air releases)
- A listing of the hazardous materials used by your company, including information on the potential environmental impacts or guidance as to where such information can be readily obtained (e.g., location of material safety data sheets)

Many of the companies that the authors have talked with have either considered or are developing integrated contingency plans (ICPs) under the U.S. EPA One Plan process. The EMS implementation process involves an analysis of your existing contingency procedures. Therefore, it provides an opportune time to consider combining those plans into an ICP.

CHAPTER 7

MONITORING AND IMPROVING EMS PERFORMANCE

7.1 Monitoring Performance through Measurements and Audits

The processes of measuring, monitoring, and evaluating the performance of your EMS are critical to top management's understanding of whether your EMS is achieving its intended purpose—that is, performing in accordance with the environmental policy in such a way as to achieve your company's environmental objectives and targets. Maintaining an effective EMS requires that you measure and monitor actual performance, identify nonconformance and take corrective and preventative action, maintain records of the ongoing operation of your EMS, and perform periodic EMS audits.

7.1.1 Measuring Performance of Your EMS

In developing procedures for measuring and monitoring the actual performance of your company's EMS, you could consider the following:

- Procedures that are in place to monitor and periodically evaluate your company's compliance with environmental laws and regulations
- Quality control processes used to periodically calibrate and measure equipment or systems
- Processes in place to ensure testing, maintenance, and repair of equipment or processes
- Whether you have developed environmental performance indicators for any of your processes or systems

- Systems monitoring or measurement procedures used for nonenvironmental systems in your company

Measuring and monitoring data should be used by management to determine those areas of your EMS that are providing successful environmental performance and those areas where the EMS is not effective. Measuring and monitoring data should provide information that is pertinent to your EMS in a format that management can use to determine environmental performance as compared to the company's environmental policy and environmental objectives and targets.

An environmental performance indicator (EPI) is a specific expression used to provide information about environmental performance. It may be used to provide information about management, about operations, or about the condition of the environment. Detailed guidance on the selection of environmental performance indicators is provided in the ISO environmental performance evaluation (EPE) standard (ISO 14031). The EPE standard will help you to develop a process to measure, analyze, assess, report, and communicate your company's environmental performance against criteria set by your management. In other words, it helps an organization understand and track, over time, how its activities are impacting the environment. Like the other supportive standards in the ISO 14000 series, it is a tool that organizations can use to assist them in creating and maintaining a viable, well-functioning EMS.

EPE is totally independent of both the internal and external auditing functions. Those functions, like any auditing function (financial, regulatory compliance, etc.), provide a detailed but snapshot view of an organization's EMS status. EPE, on the other hand, focuses the organization toward long-term, continuous evaluation and, hence, improvement. EPE and auditing functions work together to accomplish the organization's EMS objectives.

EPE relies upon the development of environmental indicators, which provide data to evaluate the company's EMS in a format that is useful to management. The concept of EPI has been used in the environmental field for many years, often to measure environmental performance for a specific media issue (i.e., air, water, or hazardous waste). An EPI is generally designed to provide a specific measurement mechanism that can help an organization document its progress toward a specific goal. Within the context of EPE, this is exactly how an EPI would be used—as a component for tracking and monitoring specific indicators that relate to an organization's environmental performance.

Much of the data needed to monitor your EMS performance is likely already available to you. Any data that you use for meeting regulatory compliance is usable in monitoring your EMS. Environmental performance indicators should rely on existing data as much as possible, reexpressing the data to provide the indicator desired. For example, if you are submitting air emissions data to a regulator as part of compliance, that same data expressed as a ratio to quantity of product is an environmental indicator.

Other sources of data include compliance audit reports, routine operational testing and monitoring data (such as daily waste stream chemistry), data generated by contractors (such as site investigations or waste hauler chemical testing), data available from suppliers (raw material chemical composition), and data from R&D or new process pilot studies.

In evaluating your company's environmental performance relative to your EMS, you should consider management functions, operational functions, and the condition of the environment in which you operate. Whereas your company has control over the management and operational functions of its environmental performance, it does not often have sole or complete control over the condition of the environment in which it is located. This is because there are usually many impacts on the environment from varied sources. Therefore, it is not feasible for your company to measure your company's impact on the global environment. However, it is possible to be aware of the condition of the environment in which your company is located and to use that information to help set objectives and targets and make other management decisions.

For example, if your company is situated in an area that exceeds air emission regulations, you may want to control your company's air emissions more closely as a means of preventing further degradation of the air quality. In designing your monitoring plan, you would not consider ambient air emissions, because they would be unlikely to provide information on only the emissions from your facility. It might be more appropriate to collect air emissions data close to your emissions sources so that you can track your contributions over time.

Using some of the objectives developed in Chapter 5, some examples of environmental performance indicators might include the following:

Objective	*Environmental Performance Indicators*
Reduction in energy use	Electricity used/hour of process operation
	Electricity used/quantity of product
Design for recyclable inputs	Ratio of raw material/recycled material in design
	Number of new processes with reduced inputs/total new processes
Reduction in air emissions	Total tons of air emissions/quantity of product

EPE is discussed in more detail in Chapter 9, in the context of using environmental performance information for internal and external reporting.

7.1.2 Nonconformance and Corrective and Preventative Actions

An effective EMS also requires that your company develop and maintain procedures that define the responsibilities and authority for investigating occurrences of nonconformance with your EMS, for taking action to correct or mitigate impacts, and for ensuring that preventative actions are taken. If the corrective or preventative actions indicate that changes are needed in any EMS procedures, those changes need to be implemented. Nonconformances, corrective and preventative actions taken, and changes implemented in EMS procedures should be documented. This may be no different from your existing governmental regulatory requirements, depending on the programs in place. Therefore, an adequate corrective and preventative action program, whether for regulatory compliance or as part of your TQM, will likely be sufficient to meet the needs of your EMS. As with all elements of your EMS, these procedures should be integrated into any existing programs.

7.1.3 Records Management

EMS records are the data or information that document the ongoing operation of your EMS and might include information related to the following areas:

- Environmental legal and regulatory requirements, permits, and notices
- Results of environmental training programs
- Calibration, testing, inspection, and maintenance logs
- Monitoring and testing data
- Environmental compliance audits, management reviews, and EMS audits
- Documentation of nonconformance, corrective actions, and procedure changes

Document control procedures, discussed in Chapter 6, focus on the documentation that provides the "how to" of performing EMS requirements. Records management focuses on the information obtained from performance of your EMS. The manner in which you control documents or records may be the same and may follow the same set of procedures. Since records tend to represent data and not procedures, they are used very differently. Therefore, their storage and retrieval requirements may call for more frequent and timely access. Since records consist of information that is generally needed to monitor and review your EMS performance, they need to be maintained in a format that is easily accessible for making necessary decisions. There will normally be a significant amount of data in various complex forms. The key features of an adequate records management system include identification, indexing, storage, retrieval, retention and disposal. Consider the following issues:

- The scope of your company's records collection and management requirements
- Who in your organization needs access to which information and how frequently
- How various information and records will be used, as it impacts your decision to use paper or electronic storage (e.g., data that will be analyzed and tabulated may best be entered electronically to provide easier use later)

7.1.4   Environmental Audits

Environmental audits of your EMS should include both compliance and EMS audits. Most U.S. companies are familiar with the use of compliance audits for tracking compliance with environmental regulations. Compliance audits should continue to be performed as part of your EMS monitoring, because they provide data on the ability of your EMS to ensure that your company tracks and complies with legal requirements. Likewise, a successful EMS often results in reduced regulatory impacts (through waste minimization or pollution prevention initiatives) and fewer incidences of noncompliance. Therefore, compliance audits can provide data on the success of the EMS process and can provide management with documentation of cost savings.

EMS audits are not so familiar to most companies, especially the distinction between what the EMS audit provides versus what the compliance audit provides. An EMS audit is a comparison of the manner in which your EMS elements are functioning relative to the way in which the elements were designed to function. It differs greatly from an environmental compliance audit in that the EMS audit is not concerned with whether regulatory limits are being achieved or whether regulatory requirements in general are being met, except to the extent that those requirements are the same as elements of the EMS.

For example, a training requirement might provide for training certain numbers and types of employees at a stated frequency. During an EMS audit, it would be determined whether the training has occurred, whether the proper employees were included, whether the subject matter was correct, and whether the stated frequency of training was followed. Likewise, your EMS may contain a requirement that procedures be in place to ensure that regulatory compliance is being met. These procedures might include periodic testing, regulatory reviews, and the like. During an EMS audit, you would determine whether that testing was performed, whether the regulatory reviews were conducted, and the like. The fact that you have or have not met the compliance requirements is not in itself definitive, if the procedures are in place as required. However, in this example, the EMS audit should look at the success of meeting compliance requirements as an indication of whether the procedures are working.

The frequency of EMS audits depends on the complexity of your EMS and the history of compliance with it. It is wise to consider performing an EMS audit before a certification audit or certification check audit, to allow you to address any deficiencies prior to the appearance of the external certification auditor.

An EMS audit can be performed internally or by an external auditor. The key factor is that the auditor be in a position to perform an objective and impartial audit and that the auditor be adequately trained. One approach is to have personnel from one facility perform audits at other facilities where they have no personal interest in the outcome.

7.2   Management Review of the EMS

Most organizations will not be able to implement a complete and all-encompassing EMS at the outset. Therefore, the notion of continual improvement arises. Continual improvement happens when management continually reviews information on the performance of the EMS; compares this performance to the environmental policy, objectives, and targets; and looks for ways to improve performance. This can occur through changes at any level of the EMS, from the environmental policy, objectives, targets, operational procedures, training, and so on.

The continual improvement process should allow your management to achieve the following:

- Find opportunities for improvement of the EMS, which can lead to improved environmental performance.
- Determine and understand the causes of nonconformances or deficiencies in the EMS.
- Undertake corrective and preventative actions.
- Measure the effectiveness of corrective and preventative actions.
- Document changes in procedures required by improvements in the EMS process.
- Appraise the effectiveness of its defined objectives and targets and make changes accordingly.

Your management should consider any data or information generated as part of the performance of your EMS. Management review should include the following points:

- Consideration of the environmental objectives and targets, whether they are appropriate for achieving environmental performance, and whether others should be considered

- A determination of the company's actual environmental performance over the period under review
- A review of EMS audit findings
- An understanding of the acceptance of the EMS by employees and management and the level of continued motivation for success of the EMS
- An evaluation of the environmental policy and whether changes are needed in response to changed conditions (new legislation, revised processes, new products, or expectations of outside parties) or inadequacies in the performance of the EMS that are likely caused by failure to focus on appropriate environmental aspects
- An evaluation of environmental aspects and the determination of their significance

CHAPTER 8

THIRD-PARTY CERTIFICATION

When developing and implementing an EMS, the organization must be careful not to lose sight of the fact that this is a management system being developed and not just a set of requirements being met. In order for the registration process to proceed smoothly, the EMS must demonstrate effectiveness and unification as a system, which, as a whole, meets the requirements of the standard.

GREG HANSA
EMS CERTIFICATION MANAGER
SGS INTERNATIONAL CERTIFICATION SERVICES INC.

The preeminent certification EMS standard is the global ISO 14001 standard. The ISO 14001 standard was published in September 1996, and by early 1998 there were nearly 1,000 companies certified worldwide, with almost 100 in the United States. Like its counterpart in the area of quality assurance (ISO 9000), the power of ISO 14001 is in the registration process. You are ready to seek certification when your EMS implementation has reached a point where the critical elements are in place and functioning.

It is not necessary that all of your environmental programs be completed. For example, if your training programs have been set up and training has begun, it is not necessary that all identified employees have completed training. The auditor will need to be able to confirm that you have a system running and that training is effectively occurring.

Many companies check the operation of their EMS by conducting a *preaudit* prior to seeking a certification audit. A preaudit is an audit your company conducts or has a third party conduct for the purpose of appraising the status of your

EMS relative to ISO 14001. This audit provides an indication of the likelihood that your EMS will meet the examination of a formal certification audit. It can also identify areas where additional work is needed, allowing deficiencies to be corrected. This can prevent the costs and waste of time associated with a failed certification audit. Your preaudit auditor should be an experienced ISO 14001 EMS auditor and may be an ISO 14001–certified auditor. There are numerous firms that perform ISO 14001 audits, that have ISO 14001–certified auditors, but that do not perform formal certification audits. This auditor should have ISO 14001 EMS auditor training, should have conducted previous EMS audits, and preferably should have experience auditing facilities similar to yours. However, a certification auditor can not perform a preaudit and then conduct a certification audit. Likewise, a certification auditor is barred from providing advice on how to improve your EMS, even during a certification audit.

8.1 Certifying the Certifiers

The certification process involves a hierarchy of responsibility, starting with a national standards body (accreditation body). The national standards body accredits a registrar—usually a company, but it can be an individual. The standards body also accredits or approves training courses to provide auditor training. Finally, the standards body certifies auditors. Certified auditors work for, or represent, the registrar when they audit a company. Based on the auditor's report, the registrar issues a certificate of compliance with ISO 14001 to the audited company.

In the United States, the American National Standards Institute (ANSI) and the Registrar Accreditation Board (RAB) have jointly developed criteria for each step of the process. These criteria include requirements for registrars, for auditor training courses, and for auditors. A company seeking to provide registrar services for ISO 14001 certification must be accredited by one of the national standards bodies. In the United States, ANSI/RAB provides accreditation for registrars. A detailed criteria document describes the specific requirements that the prospective registrar must meet. The criteria typically address requirements related to the following points:

- The organization of the registrar, including management procedures, decision-making procedures, financial stability, quality systems, and so forth

- Subcontracting procedures, including confidentiality and conflict of interest considerations
- Quality management, including quality system organization and operation
- Procedures for granting, maintaining, extending, reducing, suspending, and withdrawing certification
- Procedures for internal audits, management reviews, and corrective action
- Procedures for documentation and recordkeeping to control data and documents related to its certification practice and to demonstrate compliance with accreditation requirements
- Procedures for assuring confidentiality
- Registrar personnel

A registrar is accredited in much the same way that a company receives certification. The accreditation body will review the registrar's documentation and will likely perform interviews, conduct an assessment audit, and conduct periodic surveillance audits. The accreditation will be issued based on the level of compliance demonstrated by the registrar during the review process. An accreditation body auditor may also be assigned to observe the registrar's auditors as they perform a certification audit of a company's EMS

Auditors must meet the requirements set forth in ISO 14010, 14011, and 14012. The criteria used to judge an auditor's competence include such factors as the following:

- Their knowledge of ISO 14001
- Their basic auditing skill and techniques
- Their ability to interact with people and their overall professionalism
- Their familiarity with environmental issues
- Their familiarity with particular industry practices and the environmental issues pertinent to that industry
- Their ability to review documentation, interview information, and other pertinent data and assess the degree of an organization's compliance with ISO 14001
- Their ability to remain objective

In the United States, auditor certification specifically includes a requirement that the auditor must complete an approved ISO 14001 EMS auditor training course. The national accreditation body typically provides certification of auditors based upon the criteria established by the accreditation body. In the United States, RAB has established the criteria for certification of auditors and issues the actual certifications.

Auditor training courses are typically provided by private firms. Numerous firms worldwide provide auditor training courses. Auditor training typically includes the requirements of ISO 14001, general EMS auditing techniques, and some training on environmental regulations, where appropriate. A certified or approved auditor training course must meet the requirements of the accreditation body issuing the certification or approval. Auditor training courses that provide training for certified auditors seeking RAB ISO 14001 auditor certification must receive certification or approval from ANSI/RAB.

8.2   The Certification Process

The important issues in selecting a registrar relate to the registrar's understanding of your needs and its ability to conduct a meaningful and cost-effective examination of your EMS. Some issues to consider might include the following:

- *Accreditation.*   Under what body is the registrar accredited, and what is the scope of that accreditation; likewise, is that accreditation acceptable to the audience to which your company wishes to demonstrate its certification?
- *Competence to conduct the certification.*   Does the registrar have qualified staff available to perform your audit; are specific individuals identified for your audits; what is the registrar's reputation; are references from other companies the registrar has certified being provided?
- *Contract issues.*   Is the registrar cognizant of legal issues such as confidentiality and liability; are there appeal and complaint provisions, termination provisions, and schedule provisions?
- *Costs.*   Are all costs associated with preaudit assessments, audits, certification, and surveillance included in the estimate; are there any

additional certification fees; what is the schedule for number and frequency of surveillance audits; where are auditors assigned to your project located, and are travel costs included (if at all possible, local auditors should be used to avoid travel costs)?

Once you select a registrar, the certification of your EMS will typically require the following steps:

- An application procedure and contract between your company and the registrar
- An initial assessment and document review
- A certification audit
- Certification or disapproval

8.2.1   Application and Contracting

Most registrars will have some form of application process, including a contract to establish an agreement between the registrar and your company that sets forth each party's responsibilities. Your company should not enter into an arrangement with any registrar without a contract. As previously discussed, your initial discussions with the registrar concerning key issues are critical to your assurance that the certification process will be conducted in a thorough and cost-effective manner. Any agreements or promises should be captured in a written contract. Typical issues you should consider include the following:

- Costs for all phases of the certification process
- Scope of the certification process
- Auditor access to your company's facility
- Auditor and registrar confidentiality
- Consideration of potential liabilities
- Appeal, complaint, or termination procedures

8.2.2   Initial Assessment and Document Review

This step, frequently referred to as a precertification audit, provides the registrar with an understanding of your readiness for a formal certification audit and with help in planning a certification audit specific to your company. It is usually conducted on site and can include a review of such things as your company's situation with regard to the following items:

- Environmental policy, objectives, and targets
- Applicable regulatory requirements, given your operational processes
- Compliance history and, if available, EMS audit reports
- Environmental programs, including training, corrective action, monitoring, and measurement
- Organizational charts showing management levels, roles, and responsibilities
- Procedures for continual review, update, and improvement of your EMS

The audit team will try to determine the extent to which your company's EMS planning meets the ISO 14001 requirements, including how well your EMS can be understood and audited by a third party. During this readiness audit, the focus is on the planning elements of ISO 14001, such as identifying environmental aspects and evaluating significance and impacts, setting objectives and targets, developing environmental programs, assigning roles and responsibilities, and documenting the planning process.

The registrar should provide you with an assessment of your company's readiness to proceed to a certification audit. However, whereas the registrar may provide you with feedback relative to areas of deficiencies, it will not, and can not, provide guidance on how your company should correct those deficiencies. It is a clear conflict of interest for a registrar to provide both consulting and certification services to a company.

8.2.3 Certification Audit

The certification audit will be like most any other audit, except that the audit team will focus on only the functioning of your EMS. It should include a preaudit meeting to discuss the format of the audit, to meet the key company personnel who will provide assistance to the audit team (escorting, identifying personnel for interviews, locating documents, etc.), and to establish a general schedule for the audit process. This phase of the certification process will focus on the implementation of your EMS. The audit team will need to interview employees to confirm that aspects of your EMS are functioning, review appropriate documents, track procedures, and so forth. They will expect personnel not only to be aware of, but to understand their roles and responsibilities and the potential impact of their work activities on the environment.

The audit team will have a lead auditor and a sufficient number of auditors to adequately examine your facility. Larger operations typically require larger audit teams. This is an issue that should be resolved, agreed upon, and appropriately costed during the initial assessment. Depending upon the environmental expertise of the auditors, a technical expert may be included in the team. An environmental technical expert is not necessarily a certified auditor, but provides technical expertise to the audit team.

Many auditors hold meetings at the close of each day to discuss the progress, clear up any problems, and prepare for the following day's activities. Likewise, once the audit is completed you should have an informal closeout meeting to gain an understanding of the overall preliminary findings of the audit.

8.2.4 Certification Decision

The registrar will make the certification decision based upon the findings of the certification audit report. Although the auditor's report is critical to the decision, the personnel who perform the audit are specifically precluded from making the actual certification decision. You will be approved if your company's EMS is reported by the audit team to be substantially in conformance with ISO 14001. Minor nonconformities typically do not prevent certification. They can often be corrected immediately or can be corrected after the audit and be checked at the first surveillance audit.

A major nonconformity can result in an overall finding of nonconformance and will prevent certification until correction of the nonconformance is verified by a subsequent audit. Likewise, a sufficient number of minor nonconformities can also result in an overall finding of nonconformity.

If your company's EMS is found to be in compliance with ISO 14001, you will be issued a certificate of compliance by the registrar. The auditor can not and will not issue a certification. The auditor will prepare a report for review by the registrar. The registrar will make a decision as to the conformity of your EMS to the ISO 14001 requirements and will take action accordingly.

In the U.S. accreditation and certification process, there are provisions for complaints to be lodged with the accreditation body against registrars. However, disputes arising over audit findings or the certification assessment must be addressed between the registrar and your company. As previously discussed, your company's contract with the registrar should address the resolution of disputes, specifically disagreements with the findings. The ANSI/RAB accreditation criteria require that registrars have procedures in place to handle disputes.

8.3   Keeping Your Certification

Once your company's EMS has been certified, the registrar will conduct periodic surveillance audits. These audits will focus on broader issues, such as your company's internal EMS audits, management reviews, effectiveness of corrective actions, correction of deficiencies noted in earlier audits, and continual improvement activities. In addition to surveillance audits, full reaudits are typically required on a periodic basis.

In the United States, surveillance audits are required at least once per year, with a reaudit every three years. If a reaudit is not to take place within three years, then surveillance audits are required twice per year and must, over a three-year period, cover all aspects of your EMS. Reaudits are required whenever your company has a change of registrar.

When you make significant changes to your EMS, it may impact your certification. Whether your company's EMS requires recertification or reauditing because of a change depends upon the magnitude of the change. Minor changes can be addressed during the next regularly scheduled surveillance audit or reaudit. Major changes may require an immediate reaudit. Your contract with your registrar should address how this issue is typically handled by the registrar and should provide as much specific procedural detail as possible. Certainly you will need to contact your registrar when changes are made to your EMS.

Likewise, ISO 14001 will likely be modified, as it undergoes formal review every five years. Typically, changes to ISO 14001, once formally approved and published by ISO, would need to be implemented in a reasonable time and would then become a subject for your periodic surveillance audits or reaudits.

Any changes to the standard would include provisions for the adoption of these changes by companies already certified to ISO 14001, including deadlines.

Similarly, the failure of a registrar to maintain its accreditation can impact those firms who have received certification from that registrar. A new registrar will have the duty to perform a full audit of your EMS and issue a new certification. During the period between the time your current registrar loses its accreditation and your certification by a new registrar, the value of your certification is questionable. As much as anything, this becomes a market issue, and its impact may depend upon the understanding of your customers regarding a circumstance that is outside your control. The issue raises another good reason for being careful and thorough in your selection of a registrar.

8.4 Certification Experience

SGS International Certification Services conducted 16 of the early ISO 14001 certification audits, starting as early as the draft standard. The experiences of one of its lead auditors, Greg Hansa, provides interesting insight into the most common problem areas encountered during EMS audits and into the expectations of the audit team.

SGS uses the two-phase audit process. The first phase of the audit process (precertification audit) is used by the audit team to determine whether the company has appropriately planned its EMS to be consistent with ISO 14001. The preregistration audit, therefore, looks most closely at the planning elements: aspects identification and evaluation, objectives and targets, environmental programs, roles and responsibilities, and so forth. The audit team also collects the information needed to adequately plan for the certification audit.

Nonconformances are not formally raised by SGS during the precertification audit; however, the audit team will raise issues that the company can address prior to the certification audit. The certification audit concentrates on the implementation of the EMS and compares the planning information provided in the precertification audit to the actual EMS as implemented. During the certification audit, the audit team's emphasis is on the available information concerning implementation: EMS implementation records, interviews with company personnel, training, measuring and monitoring, corrective action, and so forth. Nonconformances are formally cited during the certification audit.

The experience of SGS shows that during the preregistration audit the greatest numbers of nonconformances relate to environmental aspects (Section 4.3.1) and EMS documentation (Section 4.4.4). The environmental aspects concept is relatively new to most companies, and it is often difficult to determine the extent to which this requirement must be taken. A company cannot identify every aspect of its operations. There is some finite limit to what needs to be considered. SGS auditors generally expect the following aspects to be considered as significant, requiring appropriate operational controls and monitoring:

- Those directly related to a policy commitment
- Those not in compliance with a regulatory requirement
- Those having a legal or regulatory requirement involving reporting requirements or threshold limits for reportability and so forth
- Those identified as having real or potential significant impact

Documentation is specifically required by ISO 14001 in only four cases:

1. Environmental policy (Section 4.2.e)
2. Objectives and targets (Section 4.3.3)
3. Monitoring and measurement procedures (Section 4.5.1)
4. Procedures for evaluating compliance with legislation and regulatory requirements

Procedural documentation is referenced in Section 4.4.4 (EMS Documentation), which states:

> *The organization shall establish and maintain information,* in paper or electronic form, *to*
> > *a) describe the* core elements *of the management system and their interaction;*
> > *b) provide direction to related documentation [emphasis added].*

It is also mentioned in Section 4.4.6a (Operational Control), which, relative to ensuring that activities associated with environmental aspects are carried out, states:

establishing and maintaining documented procedures *to cover situations where their absence could lead to deviations from the environmental policy and the objectives and targets [emphasis added].*

Although Section 4.4.6 seems to be clear as to operational procedures, Section 4.4.4 introduces the term *core elements*. The definition of a core element is not provided; however, most EMS professionals would likely assume the core elements to be the numbered elements of ISO 14001. This notwithstanding, during the drafting of ISO 14001, the term *documented* was intentionally not included in most clauses of the standard. When dealing with elements where documentation is not specifically required, SGS auditors will confirm, where possible, that all procedures, whether documented or not, are uniformly and effectively understood by the appropriate personnel.

In general, when the audit team is dealing with a procedure that has been documented, they need only confirm that the procedure has been implemented. When a procedure is not documented, the SGS audit team will determine through interviews with appropriate company personnel that the procedure is the standard for operation and that the company personnel understand the procedure and perform accordingly.

During the certification audit, nonconformances will be formally cited and will impact the ability of the registrar to issue a certification. Figure 8.1 shows the total number of nonconformances identified by SGS auditors during 16 ISO 14001 registration audits, by ISO 14001 section. The greatest numbers of total nonconformances fall in three general areas: training (Section 4.4.2), operational control (Section 4.4.6), and checking and corrective action (Section 4.5). As discussed earlier in this chapter, a major nonconformance can preclude certification, while a minor nonconformance, if corrected in a timely manner, may not. Figure 8.2 shows the same total broken out as to minor and major nonconformances, and indicates that the three major areas of greatest nonconformances shown in Figure 8.1 account for the greatest numbers of both minor and major nonconformances. The one exception is Section 4.5.3 (Records), which has the second highest number of total nonconformances, but they have all been minor. As shown in Figure 8.2, most of the nonconformances have been minor.

The operational control nonconformances resulted primarily from problems in identifying appropriate controls within the EMS. Even though opera-

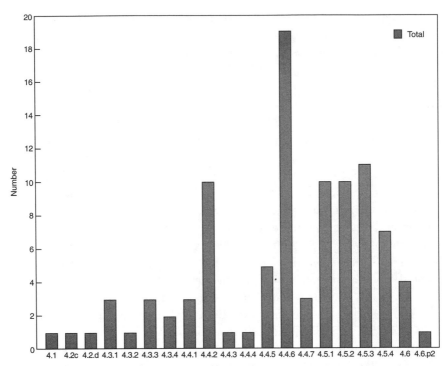

FIGURE 8.1. Total nonconformances by section. (*Source:* SGS International Certification Services.)

tional controls were frequently in place, they were not adequately identified and defined in the EMS. Operational controls included any identified systems, activities, or equipment that were intended to control the impacts associated with significant environmental aspects (e.g., a written operating procedure, a drip pan under a leaking valve, a vent over a solvent tank, or a low-flow water valve).

The checking and corrective actions nonconformances point out the need to ensure that your EMS adequately catches and corrects problems. The issue starts with the ability to measure performance, then requires that you monitor performance, in a manner sufficient to identify a problem, and have the procedures in place to respond to the problem. Finally, the EMS must have adequate procedures to prevent a reoccurrence of the problem. This was a

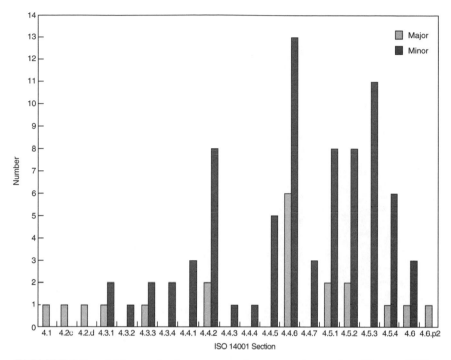

FIGURE 8.2. Major and minor nonconformances by section. (*Source:* SGS International Certification Services.)

common problem area in ISO 9000, and the SGS data indicate that the problem persists with ISO 14001. An EMS is a management tool and, as such, must be able to proactively identify problems and opportunities for improvement. Therefore, the effectiveness of the corrective action and preventative action system is carefully reviewed by the SGS audit team before certification is recommended.

One final insight from the SGS experience thus far: The number of nonconformance issues identified by the SGS auditors during the certification audits has been, on average, 30 percent less than the number of issues found during the precertification audits. This indicates a real value in using a two-step audit process, wherein a company has the opportunity to correct, refine, or improve its EMS between the two steps of the audit process.

CHAPTER 9

MEASURING AND REPORTING ENVIRONMENTAL PERFORMANCE

Environmental performance evaluation (EPE) . . . helps the management of an organization to assess the status of its environmental performance and to identify areas for improvement as needed. EPE is an ongoing process of collection and assessment of data and information to provide a current evaluation of performance, as well as performance trends over time.

ENVIRONMENTAL MANAGEMENT—
ENVIRONMENTAL PERFORMANCE EVALUATION—GUIDELINES
ISO/DIS 14031

Environmental performance information can be reported internally, externally, or both. Internal reporting is essential to the effective operation of your company's EMS. Internally communicating your environmental performance successes and failures, as determined through the environmental performance evaluation (EPE) process, has the following benefits:

- It allows the organization to demonstrate a commitment to environmental improvement.
- It allows employees to understand your company's progress toward environmental performance improvement and their role in the process.
- It allows your company to increase awareness and understanding of its environmental policy, objectives, and targets,
- It allows employees with specific roles in your EMS to understand the degree to which their efforts are successful and where more or different emphasis is needed.

- It allows management to understand the degree to which environmental programs are successful and to assess the environmental policy, objectives, and targets.

Your company may want to consider reporting to employees such information as the following:

- Cost savings resulting from environmental improvement initiatives
- Results of environmental performance tracking over time
- Recommended opportunities for improvements in environmental performance
- Modifications made to your environmental policy, environmental objectives and targets, environmental programs, or other elements of your EMS as a result of reviewing EPE information.

This type of information ensures that employees remain aware of the ongoing EMS process and allows them to have the information they need to carry out their responsibilities effectively under the EMS. Companies that have taken the effort to implement an EMS will have processes in place to report environmental performance information internally.

The more difficult question for many companies is the issue of external reporting. The command-and-control atmosphere in the United States over the past 30 years left many companies wary of reporting anything quantitative concerning their environmental performance unless required to do so by law. This attitude is understandable given that disclosure of environmental mishaps can lead to significant financial and criminal penalties. Neighbors and environmental groups have had their own share of mistrust and misunderstanding toward industry. Consequently, companies have been reluctant to discuss their impacts on the environment. However, this attitude is changing and more and more companies have discovered real benefits from external reporting of environmental performance information.

9.1 Issues in Corporate Environmental Reporting

Since 1990, the authors have observed a significant increase in the issuance of voluntary environmental reports by industry, most notably by the larger, multinational firms, and commonly issued at two-year intervals. Douglas Lober, former faculty member at Duke University's Nicholas School of the Environment and the Fuqua School of Business, has extensively studied corporate reporting trends over several years. Lober's research has indicated that by 1995 approximately 120 large public U.S. firms, representing nearly 20 percent of selected industries from the Standard & Poor 500 and the Fortune 500, issued corporate environmental reports. A 1994 KPMG environmental management survey (KPMG, 1996) of 428 Canadian companies (of all sizes and multiple industry sectors) revealed that 60 percent of responding companies prepared environmental reports of some type, though not all were necessarily intended for full public distribution. By 1996 the number of Canadian companies preparing reports rose to 76 percent of all survey respondents (KPMG, 1996).

An International Survey of Environmental Reporting was conducted in 1996 by KPMG Bohlins Environmental Advisors and the International Institute for Industrial Environmental Economics at Lund University, Sweden. Over 900 companies from the United States, Canada, New Zealand, Australia, the United Kingdom, and 15 European countries were surveyed. 71 percent mentioned the environment in their corporate annual report, up from 58 percent in 1993, and 24 percent produced some form of separate environmental report, up from 15 percent in 1993. The chemical, oil and gas, utilities, and forestry, pulp, and paper sectors were the most frequent producers of separate environmental reports.

The reasons for the increase in the public reporting of environmental performance information vary from company to company and from continent to continent. In *Coming Clean: Corporate Environmental Reporting,* Deloitte Touche Tohmatsu International, the International Institute for Sustainable Development, and SustainAbility (1993) surveyed companies and found the following major reasons for reporting: public relations, duty to the environment, stakeholder pressure, and competitive advantage. Lober's research found that employees are one of the major target audiences of corporate environmental reports, followed by shareholders, customers, government agencies, environmental groups, local communities, the public, the media, and schools. KPMG's 1996 Canadian survey revealed that employees and senior managers were the primary audiences for environmental performance reporting.

In the United States, the requirement to disclose emissions data under the Toxic Release Inventory provision of the 1986 SARA Title III law prompted many firms to acknowledge that environmental reporting was here to stay.

Corporate viewpoints also began to change due to the increased awareness brought about by the Brundtland Commission, the Rio Earth Summit, and the development of international management systems approaches, such as EMAS, BS 7750, and ISO 14000. Corporate environmental reports thus became a means to present data on a company's releases to the environment, but also presented a format for highlighting successes and offering explanations for any performances that fell short of the mark.

Worldwide, accountancy bodies and governments have also played a role in encouraging environmental disclosures. According to a 1997 review of environmental reporting by KPMG's Denmark practice, accountancy bodies in the United Kingdom, Canada, Holland, and Denmark offer annual awards for superior environmental reports, the Danish government instituted an environmental reporting act in 1995, and the force of the European Economic Community regulations (EMAS) will increase the trend already observed in Europe. Also in 1997, the European Federation of Accountants finalized a European survey of verifiers' reports and research on appropriate standardized wording for verification statements (KMPG Bohlins, 1997). The Canadian Securities commission requires public companies to report the current and future effects of environmental requirements in an Annual Information Form. In the United States, the Securities and Exchange Commission has required disclosure of companies' environmental liabilities since 1992, and guidance on characterizing, disclosing, and accruing information for contingent liabilities associated with remediation of waste sites was presented in the 1996 issuance of *Statement of Position 96-1* by the American Institute of Certified Public Accountants (AIPCA, 1996).

Most of the corporate environmental reports are purposefully attractive, with liberal use of color and graphics. Yet, most have also progressed beyond the earlier "green glossies" that were so heavily criticized by the environmental NGO community and other stakeholders for their style-over-substance approach. The best of the reports strive to combine an attractive and readable magazine-style product with useful, timely, and straightforward information. The task of producing a worthwhile environmental report is daunting when you consider that no definitive standards exist for the report's content, format or definition of terms. Furthermore, a company is in effect attempting to reach a wide spectrum of stakeholders from investors to the general public. Each of these constituencies has its particular topical interest, desired degree

> Too many companies are still treating the Environmental Report mainly as a public relation vehicle—for reassurance and "feel-good" image-building—whereas stakeholders are increasingly using the Environmental Reports as a means of comparing and differentiating between companies on the basis of hard performance data.
>
> *John Elkington, SustainAbility*

of data quantification, preference for presentation format, and so forth, and would no doubt desire a tailored report if that were possible. The company producing an environmental report, a "report card" in a sense, must try to balance the needs of these various stakeholder groups.

Baxter International reports having won more than 20 awards for its environmental initiatives in 1996 and a total of more than 100 awards since 1989. Baxter credits its reporting of environmental performance information to the public as a key factor in accomplishing this level of recognition of its environmental achievements.

Likewise, financial institutions are more savvy today and are beginning to recognize good environmental performance as having a direct impact on financial stability. Customers are also more savvy and are looking more and more for companies that have a proven environmental track record.

Although standards do not exist, several guidelines are available for firms seeking to produce environmental reports in a manner acceptable to many of the stakeholders. The Canadian Institute of Chartered Accountants has developed and issued *Reporting on Environmental Performance* (cited in KPMG,

> Swiss Bank Corporation is in the process of integrating environmental aspects into its customer rating system. This allows us to use "risk adjusted pricing" by focusing on relevant and reasonable environmental facts and in assessing risks and opportunities in our industrial, financial and management rating of a borrower.
>
> *Franz Knecht, Vice President, Swiss Bank Corporation*
> *Environmental Management Services*

1996), which states that environmental performance information should have the following characteristics:

- Be easily understood and adequately explained
- Be supported by actual findings, backed up by an audit or other verification process
- Be an adequate reflection of the true position of the organization
- Be presented in a consistent manner from report to report

One of the more definitive and widely used guidelines, *Public Environmental Reporting Initiative (PERI),* was developed by nine North American multinational companies for voluntary reporting. The PERI guidelines were developed by Amoco, BP (U.K.), Du Pont, Dow, IBM, Northern Telecom, Phillips Petroleum, Polaroid, Rockwell International, and United Technologies as a set of core elements for corporations to follow. The guidelines may not include all of the elements that a company wishes to address, or is asked to address by stakeholder groups, in its environmental report. The advantage of the PERI guidelines is perhaps their adaptability to corporations at differing levels of environmental management maturity and differing stakeholder requirements. The report content recommended by PERI includes the following ten elements:

1. Organizational profile
2. Environmental policy
3. Environmental management
4. Environmental releases
5. Resource conservation
6. Environmental risk management
7. Environmental compliance
8. Product stewardship
9. Employee recognition
10. Stakeholder involvement

Another notable private-sector initiative for reporting is the nonprofit Coalition for Environmentally Responsible Economies (CERES). Since its founding in 1989 as an outgrowth of the Social Investment Forum, CERES' mission has been to strengthen the relationship between business and the environment through the belief that globally sustainable economic activity must also be environmentally responsible. Companies choosing to endorse the CERES Principles (originally called the Valdez Principles) commit to abide by the Ten Principles, assume corporate environmental responsibility at the board of director's level, and submit comprehensive annual environmental reports. The reports are prepared by participating companies using a standardized CERES format and are then reviewed by CERES staff (but not judged or ranked) before being made available to stakeholders. CERES' primary focus is on the process of reporting, through the organization's role as a conduit of standardized performance data for investors and other interested parties.

Over 50 organizations have endorsed the CERES Principles. Some are small to medium-sized enterprises well known for their environmental orientation, such as the personal care company, Toms of Maine, or the outdoor clothing and accessories firm, the Timberland Company. But numerous large manufacturing, utility, consumer products, and financial service firms are also well represented, such as the following:

Arizona Public Service Company
Bank America Corporation
Baxter International
Bethlehem Steel Corporation
Coca-Cola
General Motors Corporation
H.B. Fuller
ITT Industries
Pennsylvania Power and Light Resources
Polaroid Corporation
Sun Company, Inc.
United States Trust of Boston

According to Director of Coalition Programs Brad Sperber, CERES believes that universal standardized reporting of corporate environmental performance is inevitable, much in the same fashion as standardized financial reporting is today. The desire of U.S. consumers for more and better-quality information to make better purchasing and investment decisions will drive the standardization process. As environmental stewards of their companies, participants in the CERES process have the opportunity to shape the finished product.

In mid-1997, CERES launched a Global Reporting Initiative designed to build a worldwide consensus on the standards for reporting and measuring corporate environmental performance. This far-reaching initiative hopes to help create widely accepted core metrics that reflect sustainability and environmental performance and eventually will link to financial reporting. Cooperating in this Global Reporting Initiative are such organizations as the U.N. Environmental Programme, The U.N. Commission on Trade and Development, the European Financial Analysts Association, the World Business Council for Sustainable Development, the Association of Certified Chartered Accounts (U.K.), the World Resources Institute, the Investor Responsibility Research Center, the National Academy of Engineering, and the President's Council on Sustainable Development.

In addition to the growing movement toward standardization of report formats and contents through such initiatives as CERES' Global Reporting Initiative, two other trends are notable: the use of the Internet to distribute reports, and the increased quantification of data coupled with performance goal setting. Several dozen corporations make their environmental reports available through the Internet, and at least two companies—Digital Equipment Corporation and Sun Microsystems—use this medium as their sole distribution route for environmental reports, with no paper copies available. Doug Lober, in his research evaluating the trends in corporate environmental reporting, found that as of 1995, 40 percent of such reports did contain quantitative goals. This figure is supported by KPMG's 1996 international survey, which found that 37 percent of all reports contained quantifiable targets. The issues related to quantifying and reporting environmental performance are further discussed in the following chapter sections.

9.2 Environmental Performance Evaluation

The development of environmental metrics has taken dual paths. On one path are the initiatives aimed at providing companies with a process for developing environmental performance information specific to their operations. The development of the ISO environmental performance evaluation standard (ISO 14031, discussed in detail in Section 9.3) is the leading global example of a process for company-specific environmental metrics. The other path involves the development of environmental metrics to be used by multiple companies and across multiple countries. The driving force behind inter-company environmental metrics is the need to have consistent databases for comparing environmental performance. This is a key issue whenever environmental performance data is being used to make fair and equitable decisions about a group of companies. This section looks at the general issue of environmental indicators, discusses some of the ongoing initiatives to develop consistent environmental measurement data, and considers the related topic of environmental benchmarking.

9.2.1 Environmental Indicators

In the macro sense, what constitutes a *good* performance indicator or index? As much as possible the indicators should have the following characteristics:

- Be objectively measured
- Be updated, or updatable, on a regular basis
- Measure the condition of assets that are important to the organization and its stakeholders (i.e., that matter and are relevant)
- Measure results or outcomes rather than inputs
- Be understood and broadly accepted
- Be used to compare (benchmark) with similar organizations, industry sectors, and so forth

Indicators tell us how we are doing. Are we making progress, regressing, or maintaining the status quo? Indicators provide a measure of performance, allow us to track systems, and form the basis for demonstrating continuous improvement. Indicators are not new to industry. Companies use indicators in all facets of business: new product development, marketing, sales, financial status, and so forth. Indicators are necessary for a company to sustain its business or, certainly, to grow a business in a competitive environment.

Measuring performance requires that you select a success measure. These measures are often referred to as *key performance indicators* (KPIs). The KPIs are used to collect trend data, which can be used to make course corrections, reinforce good behaviors, and benchmark performance. As was discussed earlier, this data forms the basis for communication through reporting, both within your company and externally to stakeholders and other interested parties.

The use of environmental indicators is no different than that of any other business indicator your company may use. Environmental indicators are merely a specific type of KPI that measures the impacts of your company's operations on the environment within which it resides. This measurement of environmental performance should be viewed as no more daunting than your company's everyday measurements of other aspects of business performance.

Because environmental issues have been largely separated from the mainstream of business management for many years and because environmental measurement is somewhat more technical in nature than other, more traditional, business performance measures, managers are frequently wary of the task of developing environmental performance indicators (EPIs). This is despite the fact that under command-and-control regulations the requirements for environmental measurement have been extensive. The development of EPIs requires only that your company express environmental data, which frequently is already being collected, in terms that provide a measure of environmental performance.

As an example, the measurement of air emissions is a regular part of the data collection programs of any company that has airborne emissions. This data is collected in terms of total mass emitted (e.g., tons of CO_2) or in terms related to a time period (e.g., tons of CO_2 per year). This same data can provide a measure of environmental performance by relating the emission to the company's operations, such as tons of CO_2 per ton of product. If management has emission reduction programs in place, this measure will reveal over time whether emissions are being reduced. Without the relation to the company's operations, the indicator does not provide a useful measure of the success of the company's emission reduction program. If production increases, for example, the increased emissions related to this increase in production could mask an overall better performance in relative emissions.

As with any indicator, an EPI must have some prescribed value to your company. Your company must have made a decision to track some aspect of its environmental performance. Typical reasons for developing EPIs include the following:

- Measuring the success of an environmental program (e.g., pollution prevention or, waste minimization)
- Collecting background data for developing environmental programs (e.g., water usage or energy consumption)
- Measuring the performance of the company's EMS
- Collecting data for benchmarking the company's environmental performance

Whatever the reason, EPIs should be developed with a complete knowledge of their intended use.

9.2.2 Intercompany and Global Initiatives

Numerous ongoing initiatives are aimed at developing environmental metrics that will provide uniformity in how companies measure their environmental performance. Early examples of the need for a uniform database include the following:

- Offering regulatory incentives based on environmental performance
- Basing investment decisions on environmental performance
- Ensuring fair and accurate company advertising of environmental performance
- Developing guidelines for company environmental reporting

The list of organizations supporting and encouraging standardized and uniform environmental measurement includes the President's Council on Sustainable Development, the World Business Council on Sustainable Development, the U.N. Environment Programme, the Canadian National Roundtable on the Environment and the Economy, the European Green Table, the World Bank, and the U.S. Environmental Protection Agency. In Europe the state of uniform environmental measurement is much more mature than in the United States. Germany has existing statistics laws that will facilitate the development of uniform environmental performance indicators. Denmark and the Netherlands likewise maintain central bureaus for collecting statistics. Given this intensity of global interest, there is little doubt that the next few years will bring some level of uniform data collection for measuring environmental performance. In the words of the World Resources Institute in "Measuring Up: Toward a Common Framework for Tracking Corporate Environmental Performance," standardization in the arena of EPIs is not only plausible, but ultimately inevitable.

CERES, in addition to its work on developing environmental reporting guidelines, has also initiated efforts to develop uniformity in environmental performance metrics. Although CERES has been advocating uniformity in environmental reporting and, therefore, environmental measurement for many years, the issue of environmental measurement remains somewhat elusive. The problem is in reaching agreement among diversified stakeholders and interested parties, not to mention the companies themselves, over what the standards should be for environmental measurement. Key to the issue is which information is most important to the question of environmental performance and how best to measure and present that information. With the start of CERES' Global Reporting Initiative these issues may begin to be resolved. By bringing together companies, investors, professional groups, environmental NGOs, and other interested parties, the goal is to develop a set of universal environmental performance metrics for use in corporate environmental reports around the globe.

The staff of the Sustainable Industry Program within EPA's Office of Policy, Planning, and Evaluation (OPPE) has developed a draft environmental performance metrics toolkit. The toolkit is part of EPA's new direction toward a performance-based system and away from strict command-and-control of outputs. The draft toolkit is the result of EPA-sponsored workshops that included regulators, industry representatives, NGOs, and other interested parties. Generally, the toolkit groups performance metrics into categories (e.g., actions, flows, stocks, etc.). Completion and review of the toolkit is expected by mid-1998.

EPA's Office of Water Management (OWM), working with several regional EPA offices, is undertaking a major project with eight states to test the voluntary use of an EMS based on the ISO 14001 international standard. Financial assistance is being provided to these states to initiate programs based on guidelines developed by OWM and published in the *Federal Register* on January 21, 1997. Based on this guidance, 21 states applied to participate in the program and the following 8 states were selected to be in the pilot program:

1. Arizona
2. California
3. Indiana
4. New Hampshire
5. North Carolina
6. Oregon
7. Vermont
8. Wisconsin

The purpose of this initiative is to promote the use of a comprehensive EMS in facilities regulated under the Clean Water Act and other statutes, and to evaluate the degree to which these systems can help bring about positive environmental outcomes in the areas of environmental performance, pollution prevention, compliance, and stakeholder involvement. At a later stage of the project, participating states will be asked to identify possible areas of regulatory or other flexibility that would be appropriate to consider for facilities that can demonstrate that they are successfully implementing a comprehensive EMS.

To support this program, EPA is working with the Environmental Law Institute and the University of North Carolina to provide protocols for the collection of standardized and comparable data from a wide variety of pilot project facilities. The data called for in the protocols are based on the kinds of information that companies seeking to establish an EMS based on ISO 14001 would generally need to collect. The primary users of the protocols will be the participating companies and state personnel managing pilot projects.

The protocols provide for a baseline questionnaire and follow-up and ongoing questionnaires. Detailed guidance for creating an EPI list is provided. The EPI list provides data in each of three categories:

- *Category 1 Measures.* Regulated emissions or discharges and regulated materials use.
- *Category 2 Measures.* Input measures, typically measured by facilities but not regulated or released to regulators.
- *Category 3 Measures.* Environmental performance indicators measured only as a result of the adoption of an ISO 14001 EMS.

The protocols provide a brief list of possible indicators and discuss the use of normalization factors. The protocols are designed for the somewhat narrow purpose of developing information on the impact of a company's EMS on its environmental performance. However, the use and refining of this data collection effort over the multiyear term of the pilot project may well result in environmental metrics or procedures that are applicable to a much wider application.

9.2.3 Benchmarking

Benchmarks are like cockpit instruments: They tell you your altitude, heading, and speed, and prevent you from flying blind. Benchmarking complements a company's business and environmental performance improvement methods, such as TQM, transformation strategies, and vendor partnering, leading to a best-in-class position in the marketplace. The use of benchmarks enables breakthrough operational improvements by identifying, adopting, and deploying the best practices of world-class organizations, and therefore it should be intimately tied to the corporation's overall goals and business strategies. Benchmarking is a useful tool for improving environmental performance because it allows your company to measure deficiencies in its environmental performance by investigating the programs and processes of other companies. It also allows your company to develop improvement programs based on those that have already been proven and to learn how other companies have modified specific manufacturing or production processes to provide improvement in their environmental programs.

The practice of benchmarking can commonly be categorized in one of the following four forms:

1. *Internal benchmarking.* The comparison of processes within the same organization or the parent organization.
2. *Competitive benchmarking.* The comparison of one organization's processes to those of direct competitors.
3. *Functional benchmarking.* The comparison of similar processes in companies in other industries.
4. *Generic benchmarking.* The study of innovative methods or technologies that can be used in a variety of business processes.

> Benchmarking is a process of comparing and measuring an organization's business process against best-in-class operations to inspire improvement in the organization's performance.
>
> Benchmarking: The Primer
> *GEMI, 1994.*

Some specific EHS benchmark areas that a company may want to consider include the following:

- Environmental reporting and public communication
- Environmental or EHS policy
- EMS audit policy and approach
- Compliance audit policy and approach
- EHS training programs
- Material and waste tracking systems
- Vendor monitoring, including waste transport and treatment, storage, and disposal (TSD) facilities
- Environmental information management systems
- Environmental accounting practices
- P2 efforts, waste minimization, and recycling
- Emissions monitoring and reporting
- Intercompany or intercontinental knowledge and best-practice sharing

When considering benchmarking for your company, it is important to consider exactly what you are trying to understand about how your company tracks its environmental performance and how looking at other companies' experiences will help you better understand your company's environmental performance or will assist you in better defining your company's environmental performance. For benchmarking to be of real value to you, it is important that you recognize that it is *not* any of the following:

- A one-time event. To be worthwhile it needs to be continuous, or at least be repeated at appropriate intervals.

- A short-term focus, or a flavor-of-the-month program.
- A paint-by-the-numbers program. It needs to be customized to your company's needs, objectives, strategies, current market position, and so forth.
- Industrial tourism! Visiting a colleague's operation and looking around or having informal discussions is not quantitative and is not benchmarking.

9.3   The ISO Environmental Performance Evaluation (EPE) Standard

This section provides a brief overview of the contents and scope of the ISO Environmental Performance Evaluation (EPE) standard. The standard was issued as a Draft International Standard (DIS) in the early spring of 1998. Final publication of the standard is anticipated in 1999. A Technical Report is in development to accompany the final standard, and will provide case study examples of how to use the standard to develop effective EPE indicators.

ISO 14031 provides guidance on the design and use of EPE for organizations of any type, size, location, or complexity. It is not a certification standard and, therefore, organizations that choose to use the standard need not and can not seek official certification of their EPE programs. The standard is designed to help organizations develop environmental measurement indicators applicable to their own use. Although the standard contemplates that EPE information can be used for both internal and external reporting, it does not attempt to develop a list of indicators to be used by any particular organization. All examples of potential indicators provided in the standard are clearly provided solely for the purpose of generating thoughtful consideration by the standard user in order to facilitate the development of indicators useful to that user.

Therefore, development of ISO 14031 has remained outside of the debate, described in the previous section, on developing environmental indicators for interorganizational use. The standard should be used by your company to develop specific indicators which will effectively measure those areas of your environmental performance identified by your management to be significant.

The standard has, by vote of ISO TC 207 Subcommittee 4 (SC 4), the group tasked with drafting the standard, been developed to be used by organizations with or without an EMS. Simply put, the standard helps a company develop indicators in three key areas related to the company's environmental performance:

- Management
- Operations
- Condition of the environment

The DIS includes main body text and one informative annex. Section 4 of the EPE DIS provides the specific guidance on developing an EPE program and consists of the following steps:

- Planning an EPE
- Using data and information
- Reviewing and improving an EPE

In addition, Annex A of the EPE DIS provides more detailed support and example indicators. Section 4 and Annex A of the EPE DIS are discussed in more detail following.

9.3.1 Planning EPE

Planning (DIS Section 4.1) begins with a set of environmental performance criteria set by an organization's management. These criteria form the basis for determining the goals of the EPE and what needs to be measured. Presumably, any organization that decides to conduct an EPE has core reasons for determining its environmental performance. These reasons could include appraising the success of an environmental improvement program, better understanding the organization's current environmental performance in some area prior to developing improvement programs, or checking the effectiveness of an EMS. In any case, the EPE program must be designed to meet the specific needs of the company's management.

The planning process addresses the procedures for selecting indicators for the management and operational areas and for the condition of the environment. Selected environmental indicators should ensure that appropriate and sufficient information is provided to management to evaluate the progress being made toward achieving environmental performance criteria. The standard discusses the types of environmental indicators. Management indicators should provide information on the organization's effectiveness in such areas as resource allocation, legal and other requirements, and training. Operational indicators should provide management with information on the environmental performance related to materials, products, energy usage, physical facilities, and so forth. Environmental condition indicators should provide information to management relative to the local, regional, national, and global environmental conditions as a context for identifying significant environmental aspects and for selecting indicators for the management and operational areas.

9.3.2 Using Data and Information

Having used the planning step to select appropriate environmental indicators, the organization must collect the environmental indicator data and evaluate it. DIS Section 4.2 discusses the various elements of an effective evaluation process and includes information on the following procedures:

- Collecting data
- Analyzing and converting data
- Assessing information
- Reporting and communicating results

The standard stresses the importance of communicating EPE results internally to assist appropriate staff within the company in fulfilling their responsibilities and to ensure that environmental performance criteria set by management are met. The standard does not *require* external reporting, but recognizes that some organizations may find it useful.

9.3.3 Reviewing and Improving EPE

Organizations should periodically review their EPE process to identify opportunities for improvement (DIS Section 4.3). This includes consideration of the data (e.g., quality, reliability, and availability), analytical capabilities (e.g., can the chosen measurement be made), identification of indicators (e.g., are they appropriate; were others missed), and the scope of the EPE process (e.g., should management be considering additional or different impacts). The review process should act as a check on the whole process and allow management to reappraise its EPE goals. If new processes have been put in place which have different environmental aspects, these need to be considered during the EPE review.

9.3.4 Annex A: Supplemental Guidance on EPE

Annex A to the DIS is intended to provide additional guidance through the use of examples and illustrations, and to elaborate on the discussions provided in the main text for those areas where it is felt more help may be needed. The annex provides additional guidance in the following specific areas:

- Identifying the views of interested parties in the context of EPE
- Selecting environmental indicators
- Examples of environmental indicators

Guidance on Identifying the Views of Interested Parties in the Context of EPE (DIS Section A.2)

As discussed earlier, the standard is intended to be used by organizations with or without an EMS. Organizations who have not gone through an EMS process may not have considered the views of interested parties or may not know how to identify those views. The EPE standard recognizes that organizations should establish some means of identifying and obtaining the views of interested parties as part of their planning for EPE. The annex, therefore, provides specific examples on who potential interested parties may be, what interests and views they might have, and what methods to use to identify those views.

Supplemental Guidance on Selecting Indicators for EPE (DIS Section A.3)

This section of the annex provides additional guidance on key factors in the process of selecting indicators, including general considerations in selecting indicators and examples of possible approaches to selecting indicators. The annex suggests a list of general considerations that should guide an organization in assessing the likely usefulness of a potential environmental indicator. These considerations include whether the environmental indicator is appropriate to the EPE criteria set by the organization's management, is obtainable in a cost-effective manner, is measurable, is responsive and sensitive to changes, and is relevant and understandable to interested parties. General considerations should be used as a screening tool for each selected indicator to ensure that the process of developing indicators remains cognizant of the overall goals of the EPE program established by the organization's management.

The annex also provides possible structured approaches to selecting indicators. These are listed as illustrative only. The standard is careful to reinforce that no single approach (e.g., life cycle) is required to effectively select indicators. An organization should develop a process for selecting indicators that is consistent with its needs. Example approaches include cause and effect, risk-based, life cycle, and regulatory or voluntary initiative. Several of the approaches use examples of indicators to help describe the approach.

Examples of Indicators for EPE (DIS Section A.4)

Finally, the annex provides examples of possible indicators for the management and operation areas and the condition of the environment. The standard stresses that the listed indicators are just examples that are meant to start an organization thinking about its own EPE program and about what indicators would be useful for that program. It is not suggested nor expected that the listed examples will necessarily be used by any particular organization. Example indicators are presented in absolute terms, recognizing that to be useful to EPE they would need to be expressed in relative terms (e.g., per time period, per quantity of product, or as a percentage) for long-term tracking.

Examples of management performance indicators (MPIs) presented in the annex follow:

> *If management's interest is evaluating the implementation of environmental policies and programs throughout the organization, possible MPIs may include:*
>
> - *number of organizational units achieving environmental objectives and targets*
> - *number of prevention of pollution initiatives implemented*
> - *number of employees trained versus the number that needed training*

Examples of operational performance indicators (OPIs) are grouped relative to inputs (materials, energy, and services) or outputs (products, services, wastes, and emissions). Examples of OPIs presented in the annex for materials, for example, follow:

> *If management's interest is environmental performance related to the materials it uses in its operations, possible OPIs may include:*
> - *quantity of processed, recycled or reused materials used*
> - *quantity of raw materials reused in the production process*
> - *quantity of water reused*

Indicators for the condition of the environment are not impact indicators but condition indicators. The standard recognizes a difference between regional, national, or global environmental condition indicators (ECIs) and local or regional ECIs. Examples of local or regional ECIs are provided for several possible areas: air, water, land, flora, fauna, humans, aesthetics, heritage and culture. Examples of ECIs presented in the annex for flora, for example, follow:

> *If management's interest is information on the condition of flora in the local or regional area, possible ECIs may include:*
> - *crop yield over time from fields in the surrounding area*
> - *concentration of a specific contaminant in tissue of a specific plant species found in the local or regional area*
> - *number and variety of crop species in a defined local area*

9.3.4 Case Studies

As previously discussed, SC 4 approved a new work item at its mid-1998 meeting to develop a companion document to the EPE standard to provide case studies illustrating how to use the standard. Delegates from developing countries have provided the driving force behind the development of illustrative case studies as an aid to small businesses. To many companies, especially SMEs, the process of developing environmental performance indicators is daunting and the concepts presented in the standard are not intuitive. The companion document will provide multiple case studies to take the reader through the process and show how the process results in specific EPIs.

9.4 Organizational Approaches to Environmental Performance Evaluation

Many progressive companies have developed their own, often quite sophisticated, approaches to developing and using environmental metrics. As has been seen, the ISO 14031 standard provides guidance to companies in how to develop EPIs that respond to the needs of a company's EMS. It has also been seen that numerous governmental and organization initiatives are underway to find standardized approaches to developing and using environmental metrics. In the end, however, it is the individual company that has specific need of environmental performance information. The EPIs developed by your company and the manner in which you use them will continue in large part to depend upon your company's culture and its approach to measurement in general. This section looks at three specific approaches to developing and using environmental metrics. Many companies may not need so rigorous an approach, but lessons can still be learned from the experiences of the companies highlighted here.

9.4.1 Northern Telecom Environmental Performance Index

Northern Telecom is a Canadian telecommunications company. The Northern Telecom Environmental Performance Index[1] is a tool designed to provide a consistent measure of the overall environmental performance of the company. The index was developed by Northern Telecom and its consultant, Arthur D. Little, to be used as a foundation for tracking progress toward environmental goals and for external communication of that progress to stakeholders and interested parties.

The index is designed to take a large amount of quantitative data on environmental performance and translate it into a single overall score for environmental performance of the company. This quantitative data is collected from each company facility, using a standardized format and the company's environmental database. The index is a composite measure of the company's environmental performance, measured against set environmental goals, in the following categories:

- Compliance
- Environmental releases

- Resource consumption
- Environmental remediation

Within each category, there are quantified parameters, as follows:

Compliance—notices of violation (NOVs) received; fines; exceedances; incidents

Environmental releases—air; water; land; global environment

Resource consumption—thermal energy; electricity; water; paper purchases

Environmental remediation—effective number of sites; risk factor

The data collected for the parameters within each category are scored based on the performance of that parameter as measured against both long-term and annual goals. The parameters have been weighted based on the relative importance of each parameter. For example, the environmental release parameters have a total weight of 50, while remediation parameters have a total weight of 12.5. Parameters in each category are compared to the 1993 benchmark data, as well as the previous year's data.

The index considers only the company's incremental progress toward its own environmental goals. An interesting result of the way the company assigns weighting is the fact that the compliance category can only get a negative score, because full compliance is the minimum standard.

The Environmental Performance Index is calculated through an eight-step process, as follows:

1. Information is summarized and data are entered into the index.
2. Environmental releases and resource consumption parameters are normalized to the company's annual total cost of sales to account for variability in production.
3. Parameters are compared to the 1993 benchmark and to the previous year.
4. Discrete raw scores are assigned to each parameter based on performance relative to that parameter's goals.
5. Raw scores are multiplied by the appropriate weighting factors.
6. Parameter scores are summed for each category.

7. Category scores are added to the benchmark level for each category.
8. A final EPI score is calculated.

The result is the overall score for the company's environmental performance. For Northern Telecom, this procedure provides a consistent method for tracking environmental performance from year to year. It is predictable in that employees know what data routinely needs to be collected and it is efficient in that the calculation process is defined and reproducible. Northern Telecom has developed computer-based applications that make the data handling and actual number crunching much easier.

9.4.2 Huber Environmental Performance Index

J.M. Huber Corporation is a family-owned company founded in 1883. With $1.3 billion in revenues in 1996, it is one of the largest family-owned businesses in the world, with over 5,000 employees worldwide. Huber is one of only a very few companies that inventory all of the environmental aspects of their operations. Huber uses the Huber Environmental Performance Index (HEPI) to track environmental aspects. The HEPI score is a measurement of the change over time of all environmental aspects of the company, using a common scale of 1,000 points assigned to a base year of 1993. The HEPI score covers the following four categories:

1. *Community welfare.* This includes potential releases and waste management.
2. *Global and regional welfare.* This includes emissions that affect global welfare (e.g., greenhouse gases) and regional welfare (e.g., acid rain contributors).

To make the world a better place, by growing an innovative, profitable company that we will be proud to tell our grandchildren about.

Company Purpose Statement
J.M. Huber Corporation

---

3. *Resource efficiency.* This includes energy, water, and natural resources production inputs.
4. *Management systems.* This includes initiatives for community interaction, preventive and anticipatory action, and regulatory and compliance actions.

The overall goal is to reduce the number of environmental aspects over time and thus reduce the potential impacts of the company's operations. HEPI accomplishes this goal by the following methods:

- Providing a systematic and consistent format for use by Huber's business units in gathering environmental data
- Developing a profile of the environmental performance at all levels of the company (i.e., plant, business, and corporate)
- Providing a decision-making tool for establishing priorities for improvement
- Tracking progress toward environmental performance goals

Through tracking its environmental performance by looking at the total number of environmental aspects, Huber has a much better understanding of its interaction with the environment. The annual HEPI score tracks the degree to which the company has been able to eliminate environmental aspects and, thus, impacts to the environment. This front-end approach is quite unique and takes to heart the very nature of sustainable production, as it is an almost completely introspective approach.

9.4.3 ICI Group Environmental Burden

The United Kingdom–based chemical giant, ICI Group, has developed a method to measure, manage, and reduce potential environmental impacts from chemical emissions to air and water. This is called the *Environmental Burden* (EB) methodology. The EB was designed to rank the potential environmental impacts of the company's different emissions, with the goal of improving environmental management and reporting. The company believes that the EB method will accomplish the following:

- Provide a more meaningful picture of the impact of the company's emissions, compared with the customary practice of merely reporting the weights of substances discharged.
- Help the company identify the most harmful wastes and reduce them first.
- Give the public a better understanding of the potential problems associated with the wastes the company produces and show how the company is continuing to reduce the waste burden.

The EB is determined in a three-step process:

1. Identify a set of recognized global environmental impact categories on which the various emissions to air and water may exert an effect:

   - Acidity
   - Hazardous air emissions
   - Global warming
   - Ozone depletion
   - Photochemical ozone creation (smog)
   - Aquatic oxygen demand
   - Ecotoxicity to aquatic life

2. Assign a factor to each individual emission that reflects the potency of its possible impact. Factors are obtained from recognized scientific literature.

3. Apply a formula based on the weight of each emitted substance, multiplied by its potency factor, to calculate the EB of the company's emissions against each environmental category.

The EB cannot be used to assess the impact of wastes sent to the land because the EB assesses potential harm. Therefore, the company still reports waste deposits to land by weight and by whether the deposits are hazardous.

In its application of the EB, the company understands the following:

- Individual chemicals can be assigned to more than one environmental impact category.
- Each chemical has a specific potency factor for each category, and these factors can differ.

- Each category has its own characteristics and units of measure.
- Burdens for each category cannot be added together to give a total EB.
- The EB approach assumes that all individual operations comply with local regulations.
- The EB does not address local issues, such as noise and odor.

The company can use the EB for each category to track and readily visualize improvements in environmental performance for that category. EB can be plotted over time to show trends. In 1996, ICI demonstrated that the EB was reduced in all targeted categories. This information was communicated with graphical presentation in the company's annual environmental report. The EB is a good example of a progressive method of presenting existing data in a new and meaningful way in order to illustrate environmental performance in emissions areas. The EB is an uncomplicated approach that could be easily adapted to most companies and certainly provides a solid base for any environmental measurement program.

9.5 Conclusion

This section has considered the basic elements of an EMS and how to develop and implement an EMS, relying on experiences of companies who have already been through the process. It has also considered the issues of certification of your EMS, should that be your goal. Finally, it has looked at how environmental performance information can be measured and used internally and externally to provide value to your company. An EMS is a management tool for better understanding, controlling, and improving your company's environmental performance. It should not stand alone, separate from the mainstream management of your company. It should be an integral part of your strategy for maintaining a healthy and profitable enterprise.

The final section of this book looks toward how companies have been able to ensure that their EMS *is* part of their mainstream business management. The final challenge is successful and meaningful integration.

SECTION III

INTEGRATION AND THE ROAD TO VALUE-BASED MANAGEMENT

This concluding section addresses the opportunities and barriers to full management systems integration, including some of the more critical factors that can drive integration. Also examined are the roles of information technology, knowledge management, and life cycle management in the pursuit of value-added routes to environmental improvements. Finally, the growing role of stakeholders in achieving value-based management for corporations today is examined.

CHAPTER 10

BUSINESS, QUALITY, AND ENVIRONMENTAL INTEGRATION

The way to make environment a business issue,
is to treat it like a business issue.

RANDY PRICE
ALLIED SIGNAL COMPANY

10.1   Integration—Easier Said Than Done

Previous chapters have explored some of the major economic, organizational, and social drivers that provide companies with an impetus to improve the way they view and address environmental, health, and safety (EHS) issues. Chapters 4 through 8 explained the implementation of an EMS based upon the International Organization for Standardization (ISO) ISO 14001 model and discussed some of the difficulties that may be encountered in integrating such a system into the company. A rigid EMS approach that does not account for corporate culture, previously established systems, such as ISO 9000, and basic business concerns, such as competitiveness and profitability, will either fail to attain its stated objectives or will certainly fall short of its potential as an agent of beneficial change.

We know that many U.S. organizations have had disappointments either with pursuing general Total Quality Management (TQM) initiatives or with ISO 9000 quality management systems certification. In many cases, general TQM programs were unfocused and had the support of senior management for only a season, leading jaded workers to dismiss them as another "program of the month." This was, admittedly, a fair criticism. Other firms approached the implementation of ISO 9000 as simply a requirement, a need to have a certificate for the reception-area wall. In many of these circumstances, implementation never really changed the organization's underlying culture and little lasting benefit from the certification effort was achieved.

In other instances, an organization's TQM or ISO 9000 program was on track for successful implementation but was derailed by major events affecting the business, such as a corporate restructuring and associated reductions in force. The reengineering initiatives (some may say mania) that affected U.S. firms in the early and mid-1990s did not always produce the promised beneficial business results and often left a fragmented and demoralized workforce in their wake.

In many firms, the cascading effects of corporate culture damage and the disruption of ongoing or planned initiatives have made implementation of any improved EHS system difficult at best. Such was the case with a West Coast electronic device manufacturer with a long history of producing high-quality products (call it "Wantko"). Faced with increasing competition from larger domestic manufacturers of similar devices and desiring to expand its European and Asian market presence, one of the initiatives committed to by this midsize manufacturer in the early 1990s was ISO 9000 certification.

Wantko was successful at establishing an ISO 9000 system at one production facility, but restructuring and workforce reductions orchestrated by its parent corporation put a total halt to serious plans to pursue quality systems certification at its main facility. Continued overseas market pressure convinced Wantko's marketing group that it not only needed ISO 9000 certification, but ISO 14001 EMS certification as well. Dutifully, Wantko's EHS group concurred with the marketing intelligence but, lacking corporate support and resources, it has struggled unsuccessfully for several years to boot-strap its way into EHS improvements and an EMS system that would come close to conforming to ISO 14001. In spite of some success with new product introductions, Wantko continues to struggle both domestically and in trying to measurably increase its overseas' market share.

The lessons to be learned in this instance are not specifically attributed to Wantko's size. Many Fortune 1000 firms have also struggled with reorganization and the disruptions caused by major downsizing actions, divestitures, or acquisitions. Regardless of size, firms like Wantko that lack an integrated management system approach are vulnerable to difficult marketplace conditions and are unable to successfully initiate actions and activities that could assist in a reversal of their poor fortunes. This is not to imply that medium-sized or smaller firms necessarily need a large EHS group or that external resources are required to develop a well-functioning EMS. Neither is the case. What is essential is a corporate culture and management system that foster an approach toward continuous improvement and at the same time recognize that EHS matters are not tangential to the organization's success but are integral.

10.2 Quality—The Great Integrator

The formalized quality movement in the United States began with a 1959 Department of Defense standard, MIL-Q-9858A (Quality Program Requirements), which specified many of the attributes of quality systems as we know them today, including applicability, program management, organization, planning, records, measuring and testing, and corrective actions. This standard was widely adopted for U.S. governmental and commercial applications, such as by the Food and Drug Administration for its Good Manufacturing Practices for medical device manufacturers and pharmaceutical firms, and by the Nuclear Regulatory Commission and the Environmental Protection Agency for their own quality management standards. MIL-Q-9858A also influenced the European national standards and the NATO AQAP-1 standard.

10.2.1 Global Quality Standards

In the 1970s, the British Standards Institute developed BS 5750, which was an adaptation of military standards such as MIL-Q-9858A to commercial applications. As the need for a global harmonization of standards became recognized, the BS 5750 standard, in turn, served as the primary initiator for ISO in establishing its Technical Group TC 176. In 1987, ISO published the ISO 9000 Quality Management System series, the first globally developed, globally accepted quality standards.

Global standards such as the ISO 9000 series have established a valuable place in the commercial world, and while they have been embraced most notably by manufacturing industries, they have relevance to the service sectors as well. Such standards provide a consistent approach to the production and delivery of products and services, thereby enhancing an organization's efficiency and competitiveness. But do standards *drive* business improvements? To some extent they can, especially if certification to the standard is a stated organizational goal. But they are largely enablers or facilitators of the improvements desired by an organization to attain a minimum level or floor.

Changing the fundamental ways in which an organization views itself and its business mission involves cultural change. The cultural change for quality in the North American industrial marketplace originated with a problem—namely, the significant inroads in U.S. markets made by Japanese manufacturing companies in the 1970s and early 1980s. The automotive industry especially felt the sting of low-price, high-quality competition from their Japanese counterparts who had adopted the quality management principles championed by such Americans as J. Edwards Deming. The resulting TQM movement in North America was a response to this competition and the business disadvantage that was experienced by the domestic firms. In addition to Deming, TQM leaders Joseph M. Juran ("Quality does not happen by accident; it has to be planned"), Philip B. Crosby ("Changing mind sets is the hardest of management jobs. It is also where the money and opportunity lie"), and others made their mark on industries seeking the pathways to improvement and profitability. And that improvement did come in the late 1980s and early 1990s as many U.S. firms successfully instituted TQM approaches by customizing such initiatives to their needs and their specific corporate cultures.

One successful TQM approach borrowed from the Japanese and adopted by a number of manufacturing companies is called *Kaizen*. The Kaizen philosophy encourages *unending* process-driven improvements in all aspects of the organization through innovation-oriented management.

One manufacturing firm that has successfully used the Kaizen approach to its business advantage is Freudenberg-NOK, a member of the Freudenberg & Company of Germany and NOK Corporation group that was formed in 1989. Freudenberg-NOK produces sealing products; sophisticated noise, vibration, and harshness packages; and a variety of molded rubber and plastic components for the automotive and other industries. Operating from 17 facilities in North America, Freudenberg-NOK has meshed Kaizen with an aggressive, lean manufacturing approach called *GROWTTH*—Get Rid of Waste Through Team Harmony. GROWTTH uses numerous, and often small, continuous improvement projects (Kaizens) to shift from mass manufacturing to lean production where workers perform multiple tasks while constantly supervising quality.

Freudenberg-NOK launched the GROWTTH program in 1992, providing its 3,600 employees with lean systems training. Since its inception, GROWTTH efforts have saved $18 million through some 2,000 Kaizen projects. In 1995, Kaizen projects reduced cycle time by 35 percent and floor space for manufacturing by 34 percent, while increasing productivity 45 percent. Additional benefits came from a 25-percent reduction in lost days due to occupational injuries and illnesses, a 50-percent decrease in OSHA reportable accidents, and a two-thirds cut in worker's compensation costs.

Consistent with its successful Kaizen approach to unending improvement, Freudenberg-NOK's 1997 Earth Day pledge, which was printed in newspapers, included the following stated intent:

- To act responsibly and carefully consider the environmental consequences of every action we undertake.
- To vigorously pursue new ways to conserve and restore natural resources, minimize waste, and prevent pollution of all types.
- To partner with our neighbors, customers, and suppliers to raise environmental awareness and to encourage sound environmental practices.

10.2.2 World-Class Quality

In 1988, the National Institute of Standards and Technology of the U.S. Commerce Department created an award for excellence in possessing a world-class quality system, the Malcolm Baldrige National Quality Award. More than just a quality award, the Baldrige process focuses on critical success factors that can drive business improvements. Named for the late U.S. secretary of commerce and quality champion, the award honors organizations that possess outstanding management systems aimed at producing excellence in business performance and customer satisfaction. From its inception in 1988 through 1995, almost a million copies of the Baldrige criteria were distributed, yet only 546 applications were submitted, yielding a select group of just 22 award winners.

The seven Baldrige criteria that serve as a blueprint for improvement follow:

1. Leadership
2. Information and analysis
3. Strategic planning
4. Process management

5. Human resource development and management
6. Business results
7. Customer focus and satisfaction

But as much as a method for selecting winners, the Baldrige process is being used by progressive companies to improve business results, to enhance their competitive strength, and to add value for their customers. As evidence, the 14 publicly traded Baldrige winners from 1988 to 1994 significantly outperformed the Standard & Poor's 500 Stock Index by 4 to 1, or a 249-percent return compared with a 58-percent return for the S&P 500.

Nowhere is this business success more evident that with the Solectron Corporation, the first Baldrige recipient to win the manufacturing award twice (1991 and 1997) in the award's short ten-year history. Headquartered in San Jose, Solectron is a worldwide provider of premanufacturing, manufacturing, and postmanufacturing services to leading electronics original equipment manufacturers (OEMs). Solectron began employing the Baldrige award criteria in 1989, and through 1994 realized an annual sales increase from $130 million to nearly $1.5 billion and an annual growth rate of its stock of 82 percent. By the time of its 1997 Baldrige award, the firm had reached $3.7 billion in sales, a 5.8-percent market share (compared to a 2.0-percent share in 1991), and a rank of 470 on the Fortune 500.

In August 1997, Solectron was selected as one of the world's 100 Best Managed Companies by *Industry Week* magazine. Seven corporate beliefs form the basis for the strong corporate culture that is the foundation of its business success:

1. *Customer first.* Strengthen customer partnerships by providing products and services of the greatest value through innovation and excellence.
2. *Respect for the individual.* Emphasize employee dignity, equality, and individual growth.
3. *Quality.* Execute with excellence. Drive to six-sigma capability in all key processes. Exceed customer expectations.
4. *Supplier partnerships.* Emphasize communication, training, measurement, and recognition.

5. *Business ethics.*   Conduct our business with uncompromising integrity.
6. *Shareholder value.*   Optimize business results through continuous improvement.
7. *Social responsibility.*   Be an asset to our community.

Solectron's focus on quality does not stop with the Baldrige process. The firm's 18 worldwide manufacturing facilities are certified to ISO 9000 standards. Solectron believes that the discipline of the ISO registration process, reinforced by semiannual audits and recertification every three years, complements the quality results rigor of the Baldrige criteria. Since 1991, the company has been honored with 5 other governmental and customer quality awards, as well as more than 100 quality and service awards from customers. The firm has won several environmental awards, and Solectron France was the first French company to have its EMAS system certified by the European Economic Committee.

As demonstrated by the example of Solectron and the 14 publicly traded Baldrige winners just cited, the 7 broad criteria of the award translate to success by those organizations that following these precepts. Success could not have come from merely implementing an international standard such as ISO 9000, as beneficial as that standard may be, but came from a culture of continuous improvement driven by an organizational framework designed to accomplish specific goals and reach stated objectives. Susan Malette, a manager at Digital Equipment Corporation, is trained in both production management and quality systems—a combination that was invaluable in leading Digital's efforts to obtain its first facility ISO 14001 certification in early 1997. That assessment and certification process now serves as a prototype for Digital's pursuit of ISO 14001 at several of its other manufacturing facilities. Malette explains the value of management systems this way:

> *Management systems are key to continuous improvement programs—both environmental and quality. They provide the crucial infrastructure necessary for the program's support, visibility, and momentum.*
>
> Susan Malette
> Program Manager, Digital Equipment Corporation
> High Volume Manufacturing Operation

Any EHS management system chosen as the vehicle for improvement cannot hope to succeed if the organization, and especially its leadership, does not embrace a culture of improvement. The principles embodied in the Baldrige Award process have full applicability to EHS management and its integration into other business functions of an organization. For a full description of adapting the seven Baldrige criteria to the development of a Total Quality Environmental Management (TQEM) approach, the reader is directed to the landmark work, *Strategic Environmental Management: Using TQEM and ISO 14000 for Competitive Advantage,* by Grace H. Wever, Ph.D. (1996). Dr. Wever, a former environmental affairs manager at Eastman Kodak Company, describes how a well-conceived and -executed TQEM program not only leads to improved EHS performance and lower compliance costs, but to greater efficiency in production, improved worker safety, and better relations with stakeholders.

10.3 Drivers, Opportunities, and Enablers—the DOE Factors

EHS is no longer a standalone function—it probably never should have been. When EHS requirements began to accelerate in the 1970s, business reacted and formed such designated positions as health technician, safety officer, and environmental manager. And these were not positions that led to a rapid climb up the corporate ladder. They were technical positions, staffed by technical personnel with training in the sciences or engineering. EHS was treated as a totally separate component of the organization, a necessary risk management and compliance function at best, an unwanted cost center at worst. Commonly, individuals who had transferred into EHS functions from other positions, R&D or production engineering for instance, found the path to corporate advancement by moving out of EHS and back into a role more central to the organization's business needs. The export of EHS knowledge to other business units can be highly beneficial to the organization, but only to the degree that EHS responsibilities are also dispersed among the organization lines. As the trend of environmental management becoming synonymous with business management continues, cross-functional training becomes a critical success factor for the organization.

10.3.1 Why Integrate?—The Drivers

What drives progressive companies to pursue effective and seamless integration of their management systems? Many factors, such as increasing regulatory requirements or the need for positioning for international trade, lead organizations to seek improvements to their EHS operations in and of their own benefit. In the authors' experience, however, seven primary factors lead the drive toward a full management system integration that includes EHS components. All are related to creating *value* within a business setting. Value opportunities, and even the perception of value, drive most business decisions.

1. *Competitiveness.* Keeping overhead costs at a minimum by avoiding duplication of both human and capital resources.
2. *Strategic position.* Using the corporate strategic planning process to affect the full business advantage of each and every functional unit to improve profit margins.
3. *Product stewardship.* Designing EHS-type requirements into products and services for minimum environmental impacts; ease of disassembly, recycling, or remanufacturing; and full life-cycle management.
4. *Supply chain.* Managing for maximum cost efficiencies and minimum risks.
5. *Risk management.* Eliminating or minimizing future EHS liabilities.
6. *Stakeholders.* Expectations, especially among customers and investors, are for a one-company approach, not fragmentation.
7. *Sustainability.* It is virtually impossible to achieve long-term business sustainability without the efficiencies inherent in integration.

The "why integrate" question has been aggressively answered by AMP, Inc., a $5.5 billion maker of electrical and electronic connection devices headquartered in Harrisburg, Pennsylvania. From 244 facilities in 50 countries this industry leader has fueled a 9.4-percent annual growth rate in a market that has averaged only a 3.8-percent growth rate (1991 to 1996). It was the first U.S. company to receive an enterprisewide ISO 9000 certification covering all 48 of its North American locations.

AMP (pronounced as one syllable, like the electrical unit) has a strong and comprehensive environmental program. Its strategically proactive approach emanates from the CEO and President, William J. Hudson, down through all units of the corporation. AMP eliminated Class I ozone-depleting substances in its global operations nearly three years ahead of the regulatory deadline and has taken the next step by eliminating Class II ozone-depleting substances well in advance of any U.S. regulations. The firm is aggressively implementing a Design for the Environment (DfE) training program to enhance the skills and competence of its engineers.

Larry Tropea, AMP's Vice President of Global Environmental Services, expresses the imperative for environmental integration this way:

> [AMP's] . . . business functions routinely incorporate EHS principles and goals into all elements of their daily activities. EHS becomes an integral part of planning and decision making . . . contributing to long-term business success. Products, processes, and performance will improve through environmental integration . . . making the company more competitive. Why integrate environment into business?
>
> - It's good business.
> - Helps grow the top line.
> - Early incorporation into planning yields lower cost, better performance.
> - Business strategies cannot be successful without incorporating EHS.
> - Identifying risks and opportunities and taking early action grows the bottom line.
> - Investors and outside parties see value.
> - Helps unlock innovation and technology.

Enterprises other than manufacturing are also beginning to understand the need for integration. The Southern Company is the largest producer of electricity in the United States, with over $10 billion in operating revenues and 5 operating companies: Alabama Power, Georgia Power, Gulf Power, Mississippi Power, and Savannah Electric. The company also has several subsidiaries and owns and operates facilities in Argentina, Chile, Trinidad, Tobago, the Bahamas, and England. Competition in the electricity marketplace through deregulation initiatives is dramatically changing both the geographic boundaries and the operating strategies of all utilities, including Southern Company.

Management realizes that with deregulation comes greater public scrutiny of the company's environmental performance.

Continually improving and reporting on environmental performance becomes increasingly important for utility firms such as Southern Company as marketplace forces affect their future economic potentials as never before. Among the company's publicly stated goals is to integrate environmental planning with business planning in a number of ways, as follows:

- An environmental plan should follow a business approach by linking the environmental policy to the business strategy.
- Environmental planning must be linked to enhancing revenue, while maintaining a commitment to compliance and improved environmental performance.
- Environmental issues are business issues. Having a strong environmental reputation is one way to differentiate the company in an increasingly competitive marketplace.
- Employees, customers, and other stakeholders continue to expect higher levels of environmental performance.
- A clean and healthy environment is an important economic development asset in the regions where we operate. Improving our environmental performance, and providing technical assistance and other forms of encouragement to other businesses to improve their environmental performance, expands opportunities for economic growth.

For most progressive corporations today, the "why integrate" question is intuitively obvious. Done correctly, integration can add immeasurable value to the organization and further its overall business goals.

10.3.2   Integrate Which Functional Areas, and How?—The Opportunities

Leading companies understand that standalone EHS functions do not meet the needs of the rapidly changing, highly adaptable, and competitive organization. In reality, an organization's EHS issues and concerns always impact across functional and organizational lines. Recognizing this cross-functional characteristic (Figure 10.1) provides the pathway for organizational improvements through EHS-business integration.

Opportunities for EHS linkages and management systems integration exist through all of these functional areas. Some examples include the following:

Human resources. Developing an understanding and appreciation of EHS issues among non-EHS workers starts with employee orientation. Is the company's business and EHS vision made clear to all new employees? Do they understand that, irrespective of their specific positions and job functions, they are expected to help the company reflect that vision and achieve its EHS goals?

Information technology. All facets of today's companies require enhanced information technology systems, and the trend is toward Enterprise Resource Planning (ERP), such as SAP or Oracle. Many ERP systems are implemented in stages, and the company's chief information officer (CIO), controller, or whomever is leading the implementation, is usually more focused on procurement, sales, or manufacturing operations. But are EHS informational needs considered early in the planning or implementation process? ERP has the potential to be a powerful integrator and will be discussed again later in this chapter.

Research and development. Is the company investing R&D funds in product or process development that is consistent with its stated EHS vision and goals? Monsanto's CEO Bob Shapiro is transforming Mon-

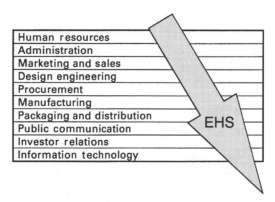

Human resources
Administration
Marketing and sales
Design engineering
Procurement
Manufacturing
Packaging and distribution
Public communication
Investor relations
Information technology

EHS

FIGURE 10.1. EHS crosscuts functional lines.

santo into a biotechnology company focused on sustainable development by redirecting its internal R&D efforts.

Marketing and sales. Marketing and sales functions should have the best pulse on customers wants and needs and should be monitoring developing trends, including environmentally driven concerns and the market for green products. Is this marketing intelligence routinely sought and are the results integrated into product portfolio decisions, for instance?

Design engineering. Are EHS managers consulted in the design stage of new products? Are they part of the design team? This is one of the largest areas for favorable impact. Design characteristics or functionality into products (DfE) that will make them environmentally benign or easier to recycle at the end of their useful life—or, as the pioneer in this DfE practice, Xerox, has shown, design products to be reused or remanufactured.

Procurement. Procurement functions offer some of the best opportunities for business-EHS integration because of the powerful position of the supply chain. The procurement process is being reinvented in many industrial sectors by companies that are serious about seeking both environmental and business benefits. The automotive industry has adopted the concept of *performance-based purchasing,* where the supplier is much more involved in its client's manufacturing operation and is paid for performance, including reduction of solvent or ethylene glycol usage, for instance. In the electronics industry, such leading companies as HADCO Corporation are utilizing *process pricing,* where suppliers are partners in the manufacturing process and are paid based on the customer's production rate. The supplier has a built in incentive to decrease the customer's material or energy waste if it improves production.

Manufacturing. In the regulatory environment of the post-1960 period, manufacturing units have depended upon their company's EHS functions to remain operational. Wastewater treatment permitting and reporting and pollution control equipment design, installation, and operation forged at least a basic linkage between EHS and manufacturing. In the 1990s, with the emphasis on pollution prevention initiatives, the linkage was strengthened but often fell short of what most would characterize as a true partnership. With a view toward building a sustainable company, new opportunities arise to create this partnership, or team, approach.

Packaging, distribution, and transportation. For consumer product companies, the creation of packaging and its disposal as municipal solid waste—household trash—has a significant potential for adverse environmental impacts. Environmental considerations in packaging design can minimize those impacts. For many companies—for instance, those in the chemical and petroleum industries—the distribution and storage process is obviously a significant source of environmental risk. Strengthening EHS linkages provides opportunities for safety and environmental improvements.

Public communication and investor relations. Does the company have a strong external communication plan for EHS issues? Are the firm's own communication specialists conversant with the corporate EHS goals and objectives, success stories, and areas still requiring improvement? Many leading firms publish separate environmental reports and have improved their investor-relations linkages for environmental issues. Chapter 9 discusses reporting issues, and Chapter 11 discusses stakeholder concerns.

Administration. Do those with administrative responsibilities in the company understand the firm's EHS vision and policies? Have their inputs and suggestions for environmental improvements been sought? When asked to think beyond beneficial but obvious initiatives, such as office paper collection and recycling, this group can provide valuable support to internal EHS improvement efforts.

As AMP's Larry Tropia states, "Environmental integration is a long-term journey." Indeed, it is much more a journey of continuous improvement than it will ever be a final destination. But that is the nature of both business and the environment.

10.3.3 Integrate Who?—The Enablers

Enablers are needed at virtually all levels within a company if EHS-business integration is to be successful and full value is to be realized.

A pioneering corporation in both EHS management and steward-ship through material management is the Polaroid Corporation of Massachusetts. The firm's Toxic Use and Waste Reduction (TUWR) program is well known within industry and is based on the premise that reducing the use of toxics and sources of other waste, per unit of production, also reduces the need to manage those wastes, thereby preventing pollution and saving Polaroid money. The program sets clear goals for reducing, reusing, and recycling chemicals and other materials, and provides a system of measurement and a formal framework that is used by the operating divisions to plan and track progress toward those goals. Polaroid's purchasing department has developed a code of conduct to use in evaluating the EHS standards of its suppliers, and the company's procurement practices include the following:

- Just-in-time ordering to reduce the need to dispose of excess inventory
- Purchasing many materials in reusable or recyclable containers, including drums, totes, and packing boxes
- Packaging reductions on shipments in and out of Polaroid plants and among company facilities worldwide
- Development of relationships with recyclers to expand the variety of materials that can be recycled from Polaroid operations

Leadership from Senior Management

Senior management can effect desired changes in a corporation. Or more pre-cisely, *effective* senior management can effect desired changes. Senior management can make clear that EHS is one of the firm's core values and is to be taken seriously by all employees regardless of their specific job titles, and can see that environmental awareness training is given a priority. EHS should be on the agenda of each board of directors and monthly operations management meeting, and business unit managers should be assigned to EHS strategy teams, corrective action teams, and DfE teams. A key success factor is to assign management accountability for EHS performance and tie compensation to performance. Not surprisingly, this tie to compensation is probably the single greatest factor that will advance EHS improvements.

As AT&T has transformed itself from a manufacturing firm to a communications and information services company, its EHS functions have been transformed as well. The EHS organization is designed to work with multiple teams across organizational lines and has designed an EHS process with four subprocesses that ensure business integration. AT&T was an early proponent of industrial ecology. The firm's Vice President of EHS since late 1996, Braden Allenby, is a recognized environmental author in industrial ecology and serves on the Advisory Committee of the U.N. Environmental Programme Working Group on Product Design for Sustainability.

Armstrong World Industries, the $2-billion Pennsylvania-based maker of finishing materials for residential and commercial buildings, devotes two pages of its annual financial report to present EHS issues. While many Fortune 1000 companies now produce separate annual or biannual environmental reports, few mention environment goals, policies, and performance matters in their corporate financial reports. If environment is mentioned at all, it is with regard to contingent liabilities for site remediations and other information that must be disclosed to conform to accounting rules.

The Armstrong 1995 annual report informs its shareholders and other readers:

> *The Environmental, Health and Safety group is rapidly refocusing its efforts to support corporate strategic business initiatives. Environmental issues are being fully integrated into all of the company's core processes, as has already been done for health and safety issues, in order to enhance environmental performance and improve shareholder value.*

Leadership from EHS

Since EHS is basically a technical discipline, its managers and staff are not automatically conversant with the language and orientation of business, and vice versa. EHS practitioners need to strive to limit technical jargon or explain technical terms. They need to be able to discuss EHS needs in terms of business drivers and be able to integrate EHS programmatic areas into daily business accountabilities. EHS can no longer serve as an adjunct function of driving

> The Federal Pollution Prevention Act of 1990 did not necessarily have a lot of teeth. Initially, awareness of business costs and process inefficiencies discovered during reporting activities, such as in the SARA 313 reports, drove EHS improvement efforts. Now, P^2 is even more important as focus turns to leaner operational costs. P^2 is viewed as value-adding and an integral part of reducing operational costs.
>
> *Jim Kohler*
> *Director, Safety and Environment,*
> *Lockheed-Martin Aeronautical Systems*

compliance for operations. The role of the EHS manager is rapidly changing, according to Jim Kohler of Lockheed-Martin Aeronautical Systems in Marietta, Georgia. Says Kohler, "EHS can't be the 'cops on the beat' anymore, trying to scare operations people into compliance. We in EHS need to speak the language of business and become an integral part of helping operations to reduce costs while achieving environmental improvements."

Companies that pursue integration almost universally have visionary leadership and usually have a strong corporate EHS group. Does integration mean more centralization of EHS functions? Not necessarily. Many companies function well with lean corporate EHS levels and sufficient staffing at the divisional or plant levels. Integration by its very nature cannot be a dictated process; it has to become part of the culture and be embraced at the lowest working level possible. Proper coordination and communication of EHS functions appears to be more important than the degree of centralization or decentralization. However, the sharing of responsibilities is a key to success. Implementing Responsible Care, or any other code of practice or management system, is not the sole domain of EHS engineers and scientists. It must be taught, shared, encouraged, monitored, and improved through EHS group leadership, but such codes or systems need to become interwoven with the company's operational and administrative functions to be fully effective.

Polaroid, AT&T, and AMP are but three of the progressive firms that are actively striving to use strong EHS leadership in the pursuit of more effectively integrating EHS into their business functions.

Leadership from the Grass Roots

"Increase the environmental awareness of each non-EHS employee" is the worthy goal of many companies. But how to realize this goal?

Baxter International's advanced work in environmental cost accounting is well known. Such efforts drive the EHS-business message down deep into the organization's structure. But training and awareness programs are also part of its arsenal. Baxter's 1995 Environmental Performance Report contains a separate section entitled "Business Integration," and regarding its future objectives, the company writes:

> Continue integrating our environmental initiatives into business objectives and day-to-day operations through increased training of non-environmental people and through increased emphasis on pollution prevention, financial benefits and other aspects of a sound environmental program.

Polaroid has developed a Total Quality Ownership (TQO) process to provide employees with effective tools for continuously improving environmental performance while also improving product quality and sustaining profitability. Employees from various functions and locations participate on Business Improvement Teams, many of which have addressed such environmental initiatives as the following:

- Organizing environmental and safety information and training for the start-up of Polaroid's new Customer Care Center
- Finding ways to reduce the discharge load on a public water and wastewater treatment plant
- Reworking out-of-spec chemical batches to make them reusable, and modifying process equipment and maintenance procedures to increase batch yields
- Reducing sample volumes to cut waste

Northrop Grumman Corporation, the aerospace and defense industry giant, has developed Environmental Management 2000, a top-down, values-based approach to pollution prevention. The program is a unique blend of technology and people-based strategies that motivate and empower employees to eliminate pollution. Northrop Grumman's environmental accomplishments to date are impressive, but they are not the result of any single, mammoth undertaking; rather, they have been built from numerous projects and initiatives—many of which were the result of employee suggestions. Since 1988, the company has reduced its total hazardous waste generation by 83 percent, saving some $35 million in disposal costs over the last few years alone. But perhaps most impressive, and indicative of Northrop's grass-roots support for environmental improvements, is its success at establishing a culture for car and van pooling as a way to achieve significant air quality improvements in the ozone-plagued southern California area. Up to half of Northrop's workers participate in the company's award-winning rideshare program and reduce automobile air pollution by 752 tons per year in the process.

The Anheuser-Busch Companies have developed strong environmental policies and practices, including the establishment of an environmental policy committee by its board of directors. But its grass-roots efforts are pursued equally as diligently as its senior management initiatives. In the firm's Environmental Profile publication, the company's grass-roots efforts include the following statements:

> *Making sure that 23,000 employees understand and commit to an environmental policy would be an enormous challenge to any company. Anheuser-Busch has found several strategies essential in gaining grass-roots support for environmental action, including:*
>
> > *An environmental professional or a team of employees responsible for environmental issues in each facility*
> > *Electronic Environmental Quality Manuals at each site*
> > *Employee training and awareness in environmental know-how and teamwork*
> > *Commitment to environmental excellence by all managers at all facilities*

Integration is a task that is certainly easier said than done, but as successful companies demonstrate, the integration of EHS with business operations is being actively pursued today. Full and effective integration of the enterprise defines the future state of a successful industry.

Companies seeking to mesh the dual responsibilities of environmental stewardship and business sustainability can take advantage of new opportunities in technology and in the advancement of business process redesign and performance measurements. Three opportunity areas that can have significant positive impacts on a company's business systems and culture are information management, especially Enterprise Resource Planning (ERP); Total Cost Accounting and Life-Cycle Management; and new performance measurement approaches, such as the Balanced Business Scorecard. In each opportunity area a strong linkage to EHS is not automatic but is necessary if the company seeks the full benefits of enterprise integration.

10.4   Information, Knowledge, and Value

We are frequently reminded that we live in an information age. No argument of course, but is this information a friend or a foe? Or sometimes both? Inaccurate information, misapplied information, or even a deluge of correct information haunt operations managers, sales staffs, purchasing agents, and EHS managers alike. In this regard, we are all in one boat and the information foe is the cause of our sinking feeling. Is it the information we need or the *buying power* that the information can bring?

In our information age, companies, like individuals, actually prize *knowledge*, not raw data—in the case of an enterprise, it is the knowledge of smart manufacturing techniques, of best procurement practices, of best pricing strategies, and of best use of cash. Knowledge puts information to effective use to return value for the enterprise. So it is not surprising that leadership companies constantly probe the questions, "What is knowledge? How do we acquire it and how should we manage it?" At the most fundamental level, companies manage *information* to create *knowledge* to, in turn, create *value*.

Just a short 15 to 20 years ago, information management systems were number-crunching behemoths run by backroom technotypes. We received our green perforated printouts weekly or monthly through interoffice mail, and that was our information management tool. The customization of reports for specialized functions (like EHS) was costly and was not commonly a company priority.

In contrast, the systems integration (SI) approach creates and automates linkages between previously isolated information systems. SI is not new but becomes more difficult as companies become more complex, diversify, expand globally, manage suppliers more closely, employ just-in-time delivery, and generally demand more from their information technology systems.

As EHS data management needs grew, so did the availability of relatively inexpensive standalone PCs. EHS functions acquired, and grew to depend upon, standalone independent systems and software packages to meet specific EHS problems. The required specialized software was either created in-house as a one-of-a-kind custom product or was a package system purchased from the growing ranks of EHS software vendors. Many of these software systems served the immediate needs quite well and became indispensable tools for managing Material Safety Data Sheets, compliance audit processes and corrective actions, OSHA training logs, air emissions data compilation and reporting, and so forth. Many of these tools continue to be used; however, this journey of independence has led to the creation of "islands" of information, with little or no ability for sharing or connectivity.

What has happened in the information technology (IT) world since 1990? The needs of business have changed, and changed dramatically. As a result, SI initiatives have skyrocketed in the late 1990s, and ERP has become a dominant trend, with worldwide annual spending estimated to reach $80 billion by the year 2000, and continued growth thereafter. Why are leading companies revamping their IT infrastructures and moving away from legacy or mainframe systems at no small cost? The answer is a compelling combination of business drivers, technology drivers, and economic drivers.

Business Drivers
- Necessity for increased flexibility to meet changing customer demands
- Dramatic business changes brought about by merger and acquisition activities and the need to integrate disparate business and IT systems
- Downsizing and reengineering initiatives forcing efficiency measures
- Rise of the *knowledge* worker, expected to be innovative and entrepreneurial

Technology Drivers
- Advantages of electronic commerce for information retrieval, technology sharing and business processing
- Comprehensive information-sharing environments through data warehousing
- Availability of high-speed connections and mobile communications
- Availability of powerful desktop workstations

Economic Drivers
- Consumption of excessive resources by legacy systems
- Overall savings accrued in transformation to client/server architecture
- Circumvention of year-2000 software problems with ERP implementation

Companies that have taken the lead in adopting such enterprisewide systems are finding that they produce significant cost savings while changing the very nature of the way business is conducted. By integrating their scattered array of standalone systems into *shared services* that consolidate financial, HR, order fulfillment, and other functions, companies are realizing cost benefits and workplace efficiencies that were previously unattainable. Data warehousing now permits companies to store, retrieve, slice, and present data in new ways to quantify trends, monitor sales data, document customer satisfaction, and so on. The *mining* of data and its transformation into strategic information drives knowledge, which leads to a more competitive corporation and one that can be a value producer.

Three factors can be viewed as the primary drivers of EHS systems integration:

EHS Drivers
- The need for compliance assurance
- The enterprisewide movement toward standardization and efficiency
- Opportunities for value-added activities

Even if we now claim to live in the Land Beyond Compliance, compliance still counts. In fact, it becomes the floor for any leading company's EHS efforts. In 1997, the EPA referred 704 environmental cases to the Justice Department and imposed $264.4 million in penalties. Criminal claims made up 278 of those cases and $169.3 million of the fines. The agency said its enforcement and settlement efforts resulted in another $1.98 billion being spent to correct violations and remediate waste sites. Many of the civil violations were the result of paperwork or procedural problems and therefore were largely avoidable. Boards of directors and executive management are increasingly seeking assurance from line managers and EHS functions that their company is in full compliance, period.

Companies are looking for information systems to solve business problems resulting from inaccurate information, information redundancy, operational inefficiency, and outdated IT functions. Multinationals especially are moving toward ERP, shared services, and standardized IT solutions that allow the organization to communicate well and operate with flexibility. Alcoa, for instance, estimated that it was using as many as 1,200 EHS software packages worldwide, resulting in large system costs and barriers to the following objectives:

- Sharing common processes and information
- Leveraging common technical solutions
- Utilizing shared services
- Establishing consistently defined nomenclature and data

Opportunities for EHS functions to add value are greatly enhanced when those functions operate as a critical business component sharing in the flow of information that serves the other business units within the enterprise. Integrated materials and waste tracking can save purchasing costs as well as waste treatment and disposal costs. Justification for many pollution prevention projects requires the ability to apportion costs among numerous operational activities and calculate a realistic return on investment. The Anheuser-Busch Companies relate the business value of an integrated systems environment to the following four process improvement areas:

1. Quality
2. Customer service
3. Cost reductions
4. Reduced cycle times

The integration of EHS software with other core business systems will typically be a difficult SI effort, but it will reap the greatest performance improvements. Companies will often have sound reasons to maintain some EHS legacy systems, but by linking those package systems with the company's ERP software, EHS information can be leveraged across the enterprise. Core business systems that EHS SI efforts typically target are the following:

- Human resources
- Legal services
- Accounting and finance
- Purchasing and inventory
- Production and process control
- Quality assurance and quality control
- Research and development
- Product or material laboratory
- Sales and distribution

The acknowledged leader in integrated ERP software is SAP of Germany, whose R/3 system was an early favorite among heavy manufacturing industries, such as chemicals, but is now being embraced by electronics and computer companies, such as Microsoft and Intel. Other prominent systems making inroads with corporate America are Oracle, Baan, J.D. Edwards, and PeopleSoft.

Do these enterprisewide package solutions offer anything to EHS? Several definitely do. Properly used, database and client/server IT solutions can maintain and manage data on all aspects of a company's EHS requirements and can help in the development of management strategies.

Oracle is a client/server application suite using an advanced relational database management system. Oracle Environmental offers EHS modules grouped in four functional areas: materials and facility management, regulatory compliance, environmental emissions, and corrective actions. This suite of integrated applications has been implemented by a number of major U.S. firms. The Oracle Environmental system verifies compliance and permit tracking, will track and forecast performance, and generates regulatory compliance reports.

SAP offers only a materials management–type module, or *function*, and in early 1998 announced that it will not develop other EHS modules for R/3 but rather will use a design analysis for interfaces to third-party software vendors. This means that a wide array of robust EHS software in current use can be integrated seamlessly with SAP.

The SI activities and EHS needs of corporations are beginning to find common paths toward convergence. Although relatively few firms have yet to commit to full EHS integration, the weight of the overall advantages will likely convince an increasing number to pursue such pathways.

ALCOA ERP/EHS Approach

Mission

Minimize the variability in Alcoa's business process and implement a purchased ERP system solution for all of Alcoa's Business and Resource Units worldwide to obtain "a common and complete suite of systems needed to run a business."

EHS Business Objectives

Efficient recordkeeping and monitoring system to ensure compliance.

Track progress against Alcoa values, policies, and mandatory procedures.

Ensure 100-percent accuracy of compliance reporting.

Support ISO 14000 requirements.

Support worldwide regional centers.

EHS Business Values

Reduced effort in MSDS and hazardous materials management.

Provide mechanism to comply with Alcoa's worldwide health protocol.

Streamline data-gathering efforts to and from manufacturing.

Nancy L. Palazzetti
Manager, Environmental, Health, and Safety Information Systems
Alcoa

10.5   Environmental Cost Accounting

A successful environmental management system should have an environmental cost accounting system and a capital budgeting process that considers a full array of private environmental cost and revenue information.
EPA Office of Pollution Prevention and Toxics—1995

The Federal Pollution Prevention Act of 1990 established a logical hierarchy for addressing and prioritizing companies' environmental management activities:

1. Pollution Prevention (P2)
2. Recycle
3. Treatment
4. Disposal

When Carol Browner was appointed EPA Administrator in 1992, she reinforced the 1990 statute by declaring that "P2 is the central tenet of EPA's activities." With that emphasis set in motion, stakeholders then adopted the stance that effective P2 was not possible without the use of environmental accounting. EPA held focus groups seeking further stakeholder input to a process that established the agency's Environmental Accounting Project. The project's goal is "to encourage and motivate businesses to understand the full spectrum of environmental costs and integrate these costs into decision making."

Environmental cost accounting, total cost accounting, full cost accounting, and activity-based costing are terms that many EHS managers have become familiar with and that many more will learn to use in the future. While these terms have somewhat different definitions, for purposes of these discussions we will consider a generalized definition employed by EPA's Design for the Environment Program's Environmental Accounting Project:

> Environmental cost accounting *is the addition of environmental cost information into existing cost accounting procedures and/or recognizing embedded environmental costs and allocating them to appropriate products or processes.*

Defining environmental costs within a corporate entity depends, in part, on the intended uses of that information, and it may not always be clear if a cost associated with a process, product, or scrap material is truly an environmental cost—gray areas are quite common. However, the value to a corporation of applying environmental cost accounting to its activities will outweigh the imprecision sometimes associated with the process.

For environmental management purposes, the types of costs can be categorized as follows:

- Direct capital costs
- Direct operating and maintenance costs

- Hidden or indirect operating and maintenance costs
- Contingent (liability) costs
- Less tangible costs (image and relationships)
- External or societal costs.

The first costs listed are straightforward and the easiest to measure; image, relationship, and societal costs can be much more difficult both to identify and to quantify. In most companies, the EHS managers intuitively know what the company's chief financial officer only suspects: The firm's environmental costs are not limited to the EHS department's budget or last year's Superfund remediation invoices, they are dispersed throughout every facet of the company's operations in ways that are not obvious.

Environmental costs are largely hidden costs. They are buried in traditional overhead accounts or are the consequence of conducting product or process design efforts without considering EHS issues.

No examples expose the hidden cost issue quite as well as those profiled by the World Resources Institute (WRI) in its definitive 1995 report, *Green Ledgers: Case Studies in Corporate Environmental Accounting* (Ditz, Ranganathan, and Banks, 1995). WRI studied the actual accounting and environmental practices of 9 participating companies ranging in size from the $37-billion E.I. Du Pont de Nemours to a $12-million specialty sheet glass company, Spectrum Glass. WRI's efforts illustrate how environmental costs can, and should, influence a wide variety of business decisions by posing four critical questions: What are the company's environmental costs? How large are these costs? Where do these costs arise within the company? How can these costs be better managed? In addressing such questions, companies can better understand their opportunities to integrate EHS decisions with business decisions and to move toward sustainability.

One of the most revealing aspects of the WRI report was the calculated aggregate environmental costs borne by some of the major multinational companies. The following five examples of environmental costs are presented in *Green Ledgers:*

1. *Amoco Oil.* Environmental costs accounted for nearly 22 percent of all operating costs, excluding feedstock (crude oil), at Amoco's Yorktown Refinery in Virginia.

2. *Ciba-Geigy.* 19 percent of manufacturing costs, excluding raw material, for one chemical additive could be attributed to the environmental component.
3. *Dow Chemical.* Between 3.2 and 3.8 percent of the manufacturing cost for a polymer-based product could be considered environmental.
4. *Du Pont.* Over 19 percent of manufacturing costs for one agricultural pesticide was identified as environmental cost.
5. *S. C. Johnson Wax.* Environmental costs for one consumer product were found to equal approximately 2.4 percent of net sales.

In the case of Amoco's Yorktown refinery, the documented environmental costs of 22 percent were an eye-opening surprise to those involved because the informal prestudy estimate was a mere 3 percent. Also, the 22-percent estimate actually understates the total costs to Amoco, because it does not include the unknown future (contingent) liability costs associated with activities such as waste disposal.

Even the relatively low environmental costs associated with the S. C. Johnson and Dow Chemical cases are at first deceiving. In the case of S. C. Johnson, the environmental costs exceed operating profit for this product. For Dow, the use of a seemingly inexpensive solvent was creating environmental challenges that jeopardized an entire product line.

Other corporations that have used environmental cost accounting as a formidable management tool include AT&T, Baxter International, Bristol-Meyers Squibb, Ontario Hydro, and Allied Signal. These and many other companies are attempting to evaluate both their direct environmental costs and the sometimes less tangible costs and economic benefits derived from

---

Environmental managers have got to understand business costs—accurate costs. The better an EHS manager can track costs accurately, the better change agent they will be for their company. Doors and windows open through accurate environmental cost accounting.

Lee Wilmot
Director, Safety, Health, and Environmental Affairs
HADCO Corporation

EHS improvements, such as avoided future regulatory costs, enhanced credit and borrowing capacity, increased production efficiency, lower material and vendor costs, and improved company image and reputation.

Used properly, environmental accounting becomes a valuable tool or technique that supports a corporation's integrated efforts at product stewardship, DfE, and full Life-Cycle Management.

10.6 Design for the Environment and Life-Cycle Management

Waste is raw material in the wrong place.

> *Annual Environmental Report*
> *Bayer AG*

Similar thoughts are echoed by Michel Porter and Class van der Linde in their 1995 *Harvard Business Review* article, "Green and Competitive: Ending the Stalemate." Porter and van der Linde express the business case that pollution equals inefficiency as follows:

> *Pollution's hidden costs—wasted resources and efforts—are buried throughout a product's life cycle. The shift from pollution control to prevention is a good first step, but companies must go further.*

In pursuing this further step that Porter and van der Linde refer to, Life Cycle Assessment (LCA) has become a method of evaluating a product's total environmental impact and cost. LCA is an accepted technique to determine the net environmental impact of a product, or suites of products, from material procurement through manufacturing; distribution; use, reuse, and maintenance; and recycling and waste management. At its core, it is a fairly scientific process, but it is not without controversy. In the early 1990s, a number of chemical and manufacturing firms undertook what they believed to be comprehensive LCA product evaluations only to have the study conclusions rejected by NGOs and others. After the Rio Earth Summit, when ISO/TC 207 took up the task of developing the ISO 14000 standards, LCA was included with the goal of standardizing terms and assessment methodologies to establish international agreement among all interested parties. The ISO LCA standard-setting process has been a long one due to the inherent difficulty and controversy, but in June 1997, ISO published ISO 14040, "Life Cycle Assessment—Principles and Framework." The second LCA standard—ISO 14041, "Goal and Scope Definition and Inventory Analysis"—is being balloted as a Draft International Standard, and other LCA components addressing interpretations are in Committee Draft form.

LCA is a scientific assessment that focuses on the environmental impact portion of products, not their costs. Life Cycle Management (LCM) encompasses the scientific, economic, and managerial aspects of product design, material procurement, manufacturing, sales, and distribution, and recycling, takeback, remanufacturing, and disposal. Practitioners of LCM, like ComEd, the Chicago-based utility company, view it as an essential tool to strengthen their long-standing commitment to the environment while providing the best possible return for their investors. The utility believes that the upside potential of the LCM approach is enormous. ComEd has used the framework to evaluate cleaning solvents, manage transformer refurbishment, and establish an improved procedure to control biofouling of condenser tubes.

Another leading practitioner of LCM is Chrysler Corporation, which has implemented a cost-focused LCM model to integrate environmental, health, safety, and recycling (EHSR) costs into the product decision-making process. According to Bob Kainz, Manager of Life Cycle Management, Chrysler believes that 80 percent of the cost savings opportunities occur at the design phase. The maker of the ever-popular Caravan has joined with Ford and GM to share in a unique facility, the Vehicle Recycling Development Center, where they are practicing the relatively new art of Design for Disassembly (DfD). The aim of this joint effort is to learn smart ways to close the production loop by conceiving, developing, and building vehicles that can be refurbished, reused, or disposed of safely at the end of their useful life.

In the areas of DfE and DfD, the Big Three automobile manufacturers are looking to do for North American vehicles what BMW has done for German vehicles, Xerox has done for photocopiers, and Nortel has done for telephones: develop acceptable and cost-effect measures to build environmentally smart products. The opportunities for economic and environmental improvements are extensive. Xerox, for instance, claims it saves about $500 million per year through DfD and the reuse and remanufacturing of parts.

Xerox Corporation's Environmental Program Goals:

- Waste-free products manufactured in waste-free factories
- Development of environmentally sound and energy-efficient machines (Green Machines) that satisfy all regulatory requirements, satisfy criteria defined by major environmental labeling programs, satisfy customer requirements, and meet the company's asset recycling requirements

DfE process enablers can promote:

- Senior management leadership and support
- Understanding of customer and marketplace environmental preferences and practices
- Elevation of environmental considerations as a product requirement
- Asset recycling management organization to assist engineering teams with recycling and environmental considerations
- Development of recycled materials specifications
- Incorporation of DfE into the product delivery process
- Development of engineering design guidelines and practices to enhance remanufacturing and materials recycling
- Development of training courses for engineers
- Development of design reviews and assessments that include environmental requirements
- Sharing the DfE ethic with suppliers

Hewlett-Packard (HP) is another pioneering firm in the use of DfE and DfD. HP's commitment to the environment includes providing "products and services that are environmentally sound throughout their lifecycles" by instituting the following goals:

- Designing products with environmental attributes
- Improving manufacturing processes
- Minimizing product packaging
- Enabling product reuse and recycling

Like Digital Equipment Corporation's AMRO facility, which was discussed in Chapters 1 and 5, HP maintains its Hardware Recycling Organization (HRO) to reclaim and recycle used electronic components and to support the firm's DfE objectives.

In recognition of its aggressive efforts in DfE, AMP was chosen as the Electronic Industries Association's 1998 Corporate Award winner and is a four-time winner of the Pennsylvania Governor's Environmental Excellence awards. AMP has championed DfE internally and externally since it began its global program in 1993, training more than 1,600 engineers around the world to incorporate DfE into their daily activities. In 1995, the company created an internal DfE Awards Competition to heighten DfE awareness and encourage the sharing of best practices throughout AMP. The awards program, which formally recognizes initiatives yielding the most significant benefits, measures the program's effectiveness and offers positive feedback to AMP engineers. It also enables AMP to quantify the DfE program's value to the organization.

Does the LCA/LCM approach also apply to nonmanufacturing entities, such as the retailing industry? The $12-billion building and home improvement consumer giant, Home Depot, believes so. In the early 1990s, Home Depot established an active environmental management program, and in the middle of the decade contracted for LCAs of different wood-treatment processes used by its suppliers to assist in making wise procurement decisions consistent with its environmental policy. In addition, Home Depot fully expects the consumer demand for green products to grow and is evaluating its responsibility to ensure the environmental claims of the products it offers to consumers.

10.7   The Balanced Environmental Scorecard

Business scorecards have evolved to become a useful EHS management tool.

10.7.1   Origins and Evolution

The balanced scorecard concept for business was developed in the early 1990s through a consortium approach led by the Boston-based Nolan Norton Institute, a research arm of KPMG Peat Marwick, LLP. An Institute-sponsored, multicompany study, cited in Kaplan and Norton (1996), "Measuring Performance in the Organization of the Future," explored the belief that reliance on traditional financial accounting measures alone (a lagging indicator) for planning and management purposes was too limited and hindered the ability of corporations to create future economic value. The corporate manager (and, for that matter, the investor and stakeholder) needed a broader array of business measurement gauges that included such leading indicators as the customer perspective, the product or process perspective, and the organizational learning perspective.

Representatives from Du Pont, General Electric, Hewlett-Packard, EDS, CIGNA, American Standard, and half a dozen other companies in the Institute's consortium met to discuss directions in innovative performance-measurement systems. One company that was examined by the consortium, Analog Devices, described its approach of using a *corporate scorecard* for measuring the rates of progress in continuous improvement activities. The consortium pilot tested the concept in several member companies and adopted the *balanced scorecard* approach organized around the following four distinct perspectives:

1. *Financial*—Traditional
2. *Customer*—Customer satisfaction
3. *Internal*—Business processes and product quality
4. *Organizational learning*—Innovation, workforce learning, and morale

The scorecard approach attempted to balance leading and lagging performance measures, internal and external perspectives, and short-term and long-term objectives to provide progressive companies with a powerful measurement system.

In subsequent usage by corporations, the balanced scorecard approach evolved from an improved *measurement* system to a *strategic management* system, and it is still evolving as businesses seek opportunities for improvement in all facets of their organizations. Several *Harvard Business Review* articles and a 1996 book by Robert S. Kaplan and David P. Norton, *Translating Strategy into Action—The Balanced Scorecard*, explore and document the usefulness of this management tool.

10.7.2 The Balanced Scorecard Applied to EHS Management

By seeking effective performance measurements and business integration approaches for EHS, companies must deal with the same limitations that traditional business functions face: How do you establish leading performance indicators, and how do you identify and enable processes that lead to value creation? The Balanced Environmental Scorecard uses goals and critical success factors aligned with critical performance measures under the four scorecard perspectives to keep company activities focused on meeting the business strategies (see Figure 10.2).

To explore the application of the balanced scorecard approach to EHS concerns, follow the issues faced by Tunk Lake Manufacturing (TLM; a fictitious name—the profile is a composite of several firms). TLM is an ISO 9000–certified, midsized, publicly held firm with a favorable reputation for quality in an established line of consumer products. The firm has a reasonably well func-

FIGURE 10.2. Value creation drives the balanced scorecard.

tioning EHS management system, but senior management is seeking opportunities to further improve the EHS functions and to better integrate those functions throughout the organization. TLM has expressed four primary objectives in seeking new approaches to improvement processes:

1. Drive continuous improvement throughout its EHS organization.
2. Integrate EHS with business operations at all levels.
3. Create hard metrics even for indirect benefits.
4. Demonstrate that EHS is a long-term, value-added orientation.

The Balanced Environmental Scorecard has the potential to meet TLM's needs in their expressed objectives, because it can do the following:

- Focus EHS strategy on improvement (excellence) and integration (change).
- Integrate fiscal and nonfiscal perspectives to demonstrate value.
- Provide a method to link EHS critical performance measures to corporate business strategy.
- Communicate EHS objectives throughout the company.

The four elements of a balanced environmental scorecard are expressed in Figure 10.3. The goals and measures are derived by linking them to the corporate strategy in each of the four perspective elements, as indicated in Figure 10.4.

How are these goals derived? Examples of possible EHS goals and measures for TLM are presented in Figure 10.5. Frequent review of benchmarks in the scorecard process (at least quarterly) will permit a near-continuous feedback loop to determine if TLM's management systems are in balance and accomplishing their stated goals. Through this formalized process, companies like TLM can quantify their goals and objectives in each functional area, including EHS, and can tie these measures to overall corporate strategy and vision in an integrated system.

Integrated is the operative word. As Chapter 3 discussed and Figure 10.2 diagrammatically expresses, a company lacking in a clear vision, business strategy, and senior-management leadership is unlikely to be sustainable no matter

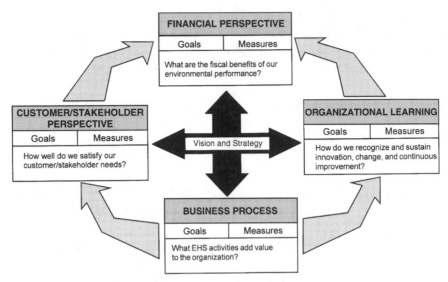

FIGURE 10.3. The four elements of the Balanced Environmental Scorecard.

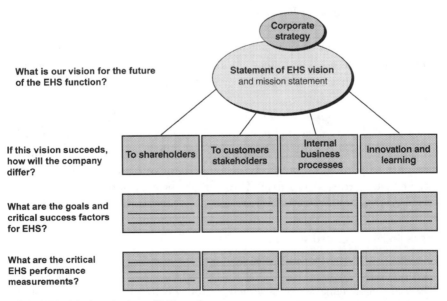

FIGURE 10.4. Linking EHS performance measures to corporate strategy.

FINANCIAL

Goals	Measures
Asset utilization	• Minimal permit waiting periods
Operating efficiency	• Tax reduction or credits
Financial leverage	• Lower overhead costs
Number 1 or 2 in market	• Reduce direct costs (e.g., disposal)
	• Reduce routine EHS paperwork

INNOVATION AND LEARNING

Goals	Measures
Facility modernization	• Training and awareness of production staff
Technology leadership	• Automating repetitive tasks
Innovation	• Number of cost saving ideas
Empowered workforce	• Staff-initiated improvements

BUSINESS PROCESSES

Goals	Measures
Risk minimization	• Reduce insurance cost
Supply chain improvements	• Waste reduction • Reduced storage
Time to market	• Number of environmental production delays
LCM	• Faster, better, cheaper
Business integration	• ISO 14001 certification

CUSTOMER SATISFACTION

Goals	Measures
Low-cost producer	• Environmental costs as a percentage of unit cost
Easy product use	• Number of product restrictions
"Green" supply chain	• Design for environment
Communication	• Percentage of recycled materials
	• Environmental performance reports

FIGURE 10.5. Example of balanced scorecard elements for EHS functions.

what performance goals and measures it sets. In such a circumstance, EHS will struggle to be anything more than a cost center and demonstrating value creation will be difficult at best. With the proper corporate strategy and vision in place, the Balanced Environmental Scorecard can be instrumental in focusing the organization on what the authors have come to call *strategic improvement*.

VALUE-BASED ENVIRONMENTAL MANAGEMENT AND SUSTAINABILITY

We have become convinced that: The quality of a company's environmental management provides the outside world with a good indicator of the overall quality of its business management.

JERALD BLUMBER, ÅGE KORSVOLD, AND GEORGE BLUM
ENVIRONMENTAL PERFORMANCE AND SHAREHOLDER VALUE

11.1 Value Creation and Value-Based Management

The preceding pronouncement could easily be attributable to a number of green investment groups, but these gentlemen are the cochairs for the World Business Council for Sustainable Development (WBCSD)—a coalition of some 120 international companies united by a shared commitment to the environment and to the principles of economic growth and sustainable development. In their day jobs, Jerald Blumberg is Executive Vice President of Du Pont, Åge Korsvold is President and Chief Executive Officer of Storebrand (Norway's leading insurance company), and George Blum is Chairman of the Board of Swiss Bank Corporation. These businessmen are held accountable to their companies and shareholders for what Chris Stinson, University of Texas accounting faculty member, terms *value-creation decisions*. They well understand the need for the convergent goals of environmental and economic sustainability to create value for their organizations.

The term *value-based management* implies formulating and managing a strategy to maximize a company's long-term economic performance—its economic value based upon revenue growth and financial return. As has been seen with the balanced scorecard approach described in the previous chapter, many nonfinancial functions can advance corporate business goals that ultimately add to a company's economic value. In that sense, value creation needs to be defined in broader terms than just those of traditional financial measures.

KPMG managers Grace Wever and Steve Chase, in researching values-based environmental management,[1] define *environmental value* in terms analogous to *economic value.* If companies assure their investors of increasing economic value by creating management strategies that result in attractive financial return and growth, they can assure their stakeholders of environmental value by creating management strategies that sustain or enhance the environment. The authors suggest that companies can create a more integrated approach to economic and environmental value management by the following means:

1. Determining the potential impacts of environmental concerns on financial return and growth
2. Managing environmental costs, liabilities, risks and threats to business performance
3. Encouraging investments in physical, human, or knowledge capital that create environmental and economic value

As an example of managing business risks, for instance, a company needs to identify how environmental issues can affect its:

- Operating margin
- Capital investment decisions
- Revenue growth
- Image and reputation
- Shareholder value

EHS functions can contribute to economic value by providing expertise and knowledge to ensure value-based investments in such areas as waste reduction, life-cycle design, procurement management, and product portfolio decisions.

This is not an argument to make environmental issues the overriding determinant in business decisions, to be applied in isolation or to the exclusion of other business factors. Rather, it is to recognize that environmental values increasingly have a positive impact on economic values. As expressed further in WBCSD's *Environmental Performance and Shareholder Value:*

There is more to creating value than getting the environmental drivers right. Despite their importance, they are only one of many dimensions a company can use to create advantage. In other words, there is always more to making a company successful than its environmental performance alone. Furthermore, the importance of the "environmental vector" relative to other critical vectors, such as innovation, employee motivation and financial control, varies from sector to sector, from company to company and even from time to time. But to ignore environmental drivers is to miss an important element of competitive advantage.

Many EHS managers intuitively know that they are adding economic value to their companies but wrestle with the following issues:

- Quantifying the value of past or current projects to the company management and its shareholders or stakeholders
- Identifying performance trends that can lead to favorable changes in the company's environmental spending
- Transferring best practices from one unit's experience to company-wide implementation
- Managing the process of prioritizing environment projects to achieve the greatest value

Even when the EHS group has good news to tell, it may have trouble communicating its message in business terms. As expressed by a corporate EHS manager at a major U.S. consumer goods manufacturer, "The [environmental performance] trends are favorable, but so what?" In other words, how do you prove to your company and to its shareholders that value is being created through all of these environmental improvement activities and the adoption of an EMS approach?

Intuitively, there should be a positive correlation between a company's environmental performance and its environmental performance—just as was noted in Chapter 10 that 14 publicly traded Baldrige Quality Award winners outperformed the Standard & Poor's Index by 4 to 1. There is growing evidence that improved environmental performance is linked to economic value, although the increases are not nearly as dramatic as with the Baldrige findings.

- Stuart L. Hart and Gautam Ahuje (1996) of the University of Michigan School of Business Administration examined a sampling of S&P 500 firms using the Investor Responsibility Research Center's Corporate Environmental Profile. The researchers found that the efforts to prevent pollution and reduce emissions drop a company's bottom line within one to two years of initiation, and the firms with the highest emission levels have the most to gain.
- A 1996 ICF Kaiser International study (Feldman, Soyka, and Ameer, 1996) examined more than 300 of the largest public U.S. companies and suggested that investments in environmental management and improved performance can lower the firm's perceived risk, with an accompanying increase in its stock price of perhaps 5 percent. These findings suggest that companies will increase shareholder value if they make environmental investments that go beyond strict regulatory compliance.
- Norway's Storebrand insurance company teamed with the U.S.-based investment management firm Scudder, Stevens & Clark to form an Environmental Value Fund in 1996. The fund invests in companies that rank among the top one-third in environmental performance within their industry sector, using nine ecoefficiency selection criteria. Early indications of the fund's actual performance since 1996 and back-test modeling analysis for the five years previous to fund's inception indicate higher shareholder returns than for funds with no environmental criteria screen.

We can anticipate that further studies of the type just summarized will strengthen the documentation of linkages between environmental performance and economic performance.

11.2 The Stakeholders' Role in Value Creation and Sustainability

Business speaks often and frequently about *shareholder value*—a fairly easy concept to understand, especially if you own any stock in publicly traded companies (perhaps that of your own employer, through a stock purchase program) or in the extensive selection of mutual funds available to even the smallest investor. We shareholders want a good financial return for our investment—and a consistently exceptional return is even better. So creating shareholder value is critical to any business—but not to the exclusion of creating broader stakeholder value. This book has explored how shareholder value is created, and several economic studies indicate the positive correlation between environmental performance or responsibility and stock price. But not all stakeholders are shareholders—shareholder value means relatively little to them.

So what about stakeholders? Who are they, what do they want, and does that get your company any closer to value creation and sustainability?

First, an obvious point: *Stakeholder* is a term that encompasses many different interest groups, each with differing needs and concerns—and therefore seeking and expecting a different relationship with your firm. Their individuality means that you cannot create a single stakeholder strategy and that conflicting needs among stakeholders are inevitable. Some stakeholders are singly focused and concern themselves with just one fairly defined issue. On the other end of the spectrum, some have a very general interest in your company and its environmental performance. Managing stakeholder satisfaction is analogous to managing customer satisfaction. As the old sales adage asks, "Is the customer always right?" The correct answer is, "No, they are not always right—but they still deserve attention and respect." For most companies, your stakeholder ("customer") list will include most of the following:

- Regulators—federal, state, and local
- Investors—individual and institutional
- Environmental groups—national, regional, and local
- Communities, including individual neighborhoods
- Customers—both direct and indirect
- Consumer advocacy groups
- Social accountability groups—child labor in overseas manufacturing, urban redevelopment, social justice, native American, and others
- Suppliers
- Distributors, contracted salespeople, and franchise owners
- Media
- Employees (last but not least)

What do these stakeholders want? For some of them, nothing more than the general knowledge that the business world is acknowledging its environmental responsibilities and acting upon those responsibilities. A *USA Today* Snapshots survey taken and published in early 1997 showed that only 9 percent of those polled consider themselves active environmentalists, while 61 percent consider themselves sympathetic to environmental concerns, and another 24 percent were neutral to such concerns. Experience shows that the majority of stakeholders from the 61-percent category, while not always specific in expressing environmental concerns, expect companies to be in full compliance; be responsive to public health, worker safety, and environmental protection needs; and produce environmentally friendly products and services.

W. Ross Stevens, management consultant with Stevens Associates and former Du Pont manager of external and environmental affairs, poses the following questions to companies with respect to stakeholder satisfaction:

- Do stakeholders recognize and value your intent, practice, and performance?
- Do products and services contribute to solving customers' environmental problems?
- Does the public see you as a problem, a solution, or not at all?

Stakeholder relationships are ultimately key to a company's long-term future—its sustainability (Figure 11.1). While your company may never satisfy all stakeholder demands—and some are actually conflicting, as has been pointed out—without satisfying most of these demands from most of these stakeholders, you will find company economic health hard to sustain and you will not be meeting the dual goals of creating economic value and environmental value.

Three very different organizations—Great Northern Paper Company, Inc., the Business and Industry Association of New Hampshire, and the Royal Dutch/Shell Group—serve as case examples of those who are addressing differing stakeholder concerns, all revolving around sustainable practices and sustainability. These examples are presented as illustrative of the wide range of issues faced by business organizations today and the creative stakeholder relationships that can result from sincere efforts at achieving the inclusiveness inherent in the concept of sustainability.

Toward corporate sustainability

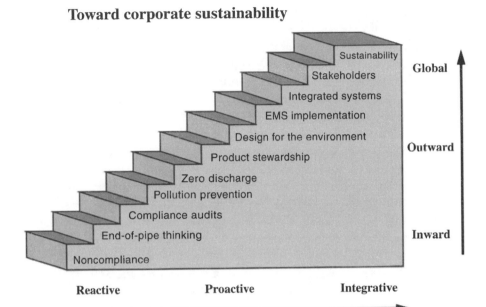

FIGURE 11.1. The progression toward a sustainable corporation.

11.2.1 Great Northern Paper Company, Inc.

Great Northern Paper Company, Inc. (Great Northern), a wholly owned subsidiary of Bowater Incorporated, is an integrated forest products company with two pulp and paper mills, an extensive hydroelectric generating system, and timber lands throughout north-central Maine. In 1997, the company produced approximately 560,000 tons of paper and 500,000 tons of pulp at its two mills. Great Northern's hydroelectric system is grouped into three projects, with each holding a long-term operating license issued by the Federal Energy Regulatory Commission (FERC). The company manages its systems to meet multiple use demands in addition to hydroelectric generation and storage, including recreation, environmental resources, and flood control. The pulp and paper industry is highly competitive and energy intensive. Great Northern depends on its low-cost hydropower resources to provide an economical electricity supply for its manufacturing operations and incurs increased costs of production when it must substitute energy from alternative sources for hydroelectric power.

One of Great Northern's FERC licenses covers its upstream storage project, a system of water bodies that does not generate hydroelectricity directly but whose storage capacity adds to the overall ability of the company to meet downstream multiple-use demands. The FERC relicensing process is a multiyear process *requiring* several stages of formal consultation with stakeholders, including state and federal environmental and natural resource agencies, commercial recreational concerns, organized sportsmen groups, environmental groups, and, in the case of Great Northern's licenses, a Native American tribe.

In spite of the required formal consultation, the hydroelectric licensing and relicensing process in the United States is often a contentious one, especially in geographic areas prized for their environmental or scenic qualities, or their fisheries, wildlife, habitat, or recreational resources, all of which are dependent upon complex water allocation and control issues. Great Northern had faced three such contentious efforts in the 1980s—two for relicensing of existing projects and one for a proposed (but never filed) new hydroelectric project.

For its last remaining relicensing effort of this century, the Storage Ponds Project, Great Northern adopted an approach of soliciting active stakeholder input by deciding in advance that the project would be operated in accordance with a consensus-based Water Management Plan (WMP). The WMP concept was designed to provide prescribed operating criteria to meet and balance the interests and objectives of the various water users related to fisheries, wildlife, recreation, and other environmental resources, as well as dam safety. The plan was developed in conjunction with an extensive stakeholder group. All interested parties were invited to participate—with the single restriction that legal counsel representing either the company or any stakeholder group could not attend.

Stakeholder meetings were held over a nearly three year period, and all participants were asked to identify and prioritize their resource concerns. Over 120 issues were initially identified, followed by a narrowing and focusing process. These stakeholder meetings resulted in the development of a variety of lake-level and flow management goals—several of which, not surprisingly, were in conflict. A computer model was developed by Great Northern to assist in the evaluation of the various desired water management goals. Based on stakeholder group discussions of the model results, a final WMP was developed that contains flow release and lake-level operating criteria that balance the various natural resource and water use goals. The target flow releases and lake levels contained in the final WMP will improve lake and stream fisheries during the growing season, increase the overwintering survival of fish in the impoundments, enhance wetlands, and improve recreational angling and boating—all at the expense of some generating capacity.

According to Environmental Affairs Manager Brian Stetson, Great Northern will propose in its relicensing application to FERC that the WMP—the stakeholders' plan—should become part of the formal license conditions for the Storage Ponds Project.

11.2.2 The Business and Industry Association of New Hampshire

The Business and Industry Association of New Hampshire (BIA) is a well-respected business advocacy group with a pivotal role in promoting and preserving the state's favorable economic climate. The state enjoyed several periods of robust economic growth in the 1970s and 1980s, fueled by expanding technology, defense, and health care industries, as well as by the well-developed recreation and tourism industry. In the 1980s, the BIA and other state leadership interests identified quality of life, including New Hampshire's healthy environment, as a clear business advantage. Preserving that balance was seen as key to continuing to attract quality employment opportunities to the state while preventing the degradation of its valued natural resources.

In 1991, the BIA undertook a business-led effort, called *Partnerships for Progress: A Business Plan for New Hampshire's Economic Future,* to define and shape public policy initiatives deemed integral to the state's future. The plan was not a business agenda. Rather, it was an agenda developed by a diverse group of businesspeople interested primarily in securing the state's economic future and preserving the quality of life in New Hampshire for its citizens. The plan began a multiyear dialogue on public policy issues (including natural resources and the environment) important to the state's future and served as an organizational tool for motivating people—the state's stakeholders—and guiding actions.

As an outgrowth and extension of its 1991 plan and the subsequent stakeholder dialogue process, the BIA developed an *Economic Opportunity Index.* The index was conceived to provide community and business leaders, lawmakers, and citizens with a comprehensive and quantitative report on the state's economic, environmental, civic, and human assets, and to serve as a catalyst to improve the economy and the quality of life. Intended to be updated annually, the first version of this index was presented to the state's stakeholders in early 1998 for comment and suggestions. In addition to presenting traditional benchmarks of educational achievements, health care, labor costs, and exports, the index, in consultation with environmental and wildlife groups, presented two nontraditional measures for public consideration: the amount of the state's remaining open space and the productivity of a species revered in the state, the loon. Loons, it turns out, are an ideal indicator species for overall environmental quality, and one that a broad group of stakeholders can identify with and recognize it as a link to general quality of life measures. As of 1997, territorial loon pairs and surviving chicks were on the increase in the state, and the BIA's efforts to reach and teach the state's stakeholders is succeeding.

11.2.3   Royal Dutch/Shell Group

This 90-year-old global group of diversified companies was stung by strong public opposition to Shell U.K. Exploration and Production's mid-1995 plans to dispose of an obsolete floating oil storage platform, the *Brent Spar,* by deepwater burial in the North Atlantic. Environmental activists occupied the decommissioned platform for over 3 weeks, while protesters in Germany threatened to damage 200 Shell service stations, and did damage some 50. Public opinion in continental northern Europe swung toward strong opposition to the at-sea disposal plans, and Germany's Chancellor Helmut Kohl protested to U.K. Prime Minister John Majors at the G7 summit that year.

The *Brent Spar* is different from any other marine petroleum structure used in the North Sea, and it presented Shell with unique challenges for decommissioning. Like an iceberg with most of its 14,500 tons beneath the water, it could not be dismantled by simply reversing the construction process. Its bulk and structural condition posed a human safety risk if an attempt would be made to raise it vertically out of the water or right it to a horizontal position. Several risk evaluation studies commissioned by Shell established that disposal of the *Brent Spar* at a deep Northern Atlantic site was the Best Practical Environmental Option, and the U.K. government publicly approved this plan in early 1995. In the uproar that occurred as the disposal date approached, Shell abandoned the deepwater disposal plan and received permission from the

Norwegian authorities to anchor the platform in a deepwater fjord until an alternate solution could be found.

Shell's response to this event was to learn from the difficult experience. The company has established a separate website for the purposes of disseminating information and receiving questions and suggestions from stakeholders. Shell's main environmental Internet homepage also discusses the company's dilemma and states:

> *Our Brent Spar experience showed us that we needed a better understanding of society's expectations. All the necessary scientific work and regulatory approvals were completed for the disposal of the redundant offshore storage buoy. But with hindsight, this was not enough because the plan was considered inappropriate by some. They wanted a broader dialogue and a greater awareness of the sensitivities of offshore disposal, and we are involved in this process now.*
>
> *Understanding the needs of all those who are affected by our activities is especially important for us as we tackle the sometimes conflicting demands of the three pillars of sustainable development—economic, environmental, and social—in different parts of the world.*
>
> *We recently completed a world-wide consultation with interested parties to get a better understanding of what society expects from us. . . . We will continue to consult widely and report publicly on our achievements, failures, and dilemmas.*

And the fate of the *Brent Spar?* On January 29, 1998, Shell announced that after evaluating several proposed options for the platform, it chose a British/ Norwegian consortium's reuse solution of slicing the cleaned hull into sections and using them to construct a quay (breakwater) in a Norwegian coastal community. The plan will be submitted to the U.K. government for approval.

Shell concludes:

> *Brent Spar is no longer just a North Sea installation, but a unique and defining event. The challenge now is to ensure that it defines a new stage in the regulation of business activity which enjoys the popular support of hearts as well as minds.*

Creating a sound environmental ethic and a path to sustainability requires the clear corporate vision that stakeholders do matter—a lot. Leadership translates that corporate vision into action and, in the process, creates lasting value.

11.3   Leadership and Sustainability

Now—in the middle of economic preoccupation and political storms—we have entered a period of testing and reaction, a time when the nation will be urged to reconsider its environmental priority, readjust the balance between resource stewardship and resource exploitation. . . . In government, as in life, there are no final answers and it falls to each generation, perhaps more often, to revisit choices and decide whether to stay the course we are on. People in many other nations are watching closely the choices we make. I expect that the envelope of possibilities will be pushed no further than we push it, that what we conclude cannot be done will be widely noticed and accepted in many fields in many countries.

"The New Environmentalism"
William K. Reilly–1992
Administrator
U.S. Environmental Protection Agency

Bill Reilly's 1992 speech to the National Press Club was an early call for leadership—from both the governmental sector that he represented, and from the broad private sector that was the subject of his agency's regulations. In Chapter 2, it was seen that Reilly, as EPA administrator, sought new means to achieve environmental improvement beyond the protection that could be delivered by regulation alone. The Green Lights and 33/50 programs marked the beginning of a challenge to industry—and specifically its most senior leaders—to begin viewing the approach to business and environmental responsibilities fundamentally differently than in the past.

Is it working? On the whole, is business' sense of responsibility changing, and does it tend to conduct its business differently today than it did in the 1980s? Evidence presented in this book, and documented by others in many published sources, indicates a clear *yes.* Marjorie Kelly, editor-in-chief of the publication *Business Ethics,* wrote in 1995 that industry's participation in voluntary initiatives, such as CERES, reflected a growing trend toward adopting *self-regulation* as integral to business operations. Kelly argued (as have others, such as Harvard's Michael Porter) that while regulation cannot be entirely replaced, self-regulation can achieve societal gains that are otherwise unattainable.

Many business leaders, especially ones known for innovation and for astutely monitoring trends, have established a new business culture and coupled it with an aggressive course of action for their companies.

Monsanto has reframed its competitive strategy of providing bulk agricultural chemicals to include genetically engineered plants that repel pests. This approach to bioengineering, piloted by CEO Bob Shapiro, recognizes that society will not accept environmental impacts that result from long-term, unlimited applications of traditional pesticides. By realigning Monsanto's research and development approach toward sustainable products, Shapiro has redefined key strategic issues and created a competitive strategy in which new products and services are generated with sustainability in mind.

Pete Correll, CEO of Georgia-Pacific Corporation since 1993, has used his personal style and vision to grow this building products and pulp and paper company while concurrently developing sustainable forestry practices, community outreach and education programs, and proactive alliances for environmental improvements and resource protection. Correll's commitment to leadership in the arena of environmental responsibility includes serving as an original member of the President's Council on Sustainable Development. One of this CEO's popular business sayings, "The world rewards risks, it always has," applies well to Georgia-Pacific's culture of aggressive environmental stewardship.

While many leaders come from well-recognized Fortune 500 firms, the drive toward sustainable development is, of course, active among numerous smaller entrepreneurial firms. The successful natural personal care products maker, Tom's of Maine, Inc., founded more than 25 years ago by Tom and Kate Chappell, is run as a values-based business with sustainability and both employee and customer care as core objectives.

Stonyfield Farm, Inc. is a $43-million, nationally distributed manufacturer of yogurt, ice cream, and frozen yogurt products that recycles more than 72 percent of its waste. Its founder and CEO, Gary Hirshberg, is seeking to go beyond the traditional models for businesses and join forces with others to create a 95-acre Eco-Industrial Business Park in southern New Hampshire that is modeled on the industrial ecology concept. Partnering with the Town of

Londonderry and EPA New England, the park's developers and supporters are seeking to attract companies whose waste products would serve as raw materials for another park tenant. Companies joining this unique industrial park would sign a covenant to seek environmentally sounder, less wasteful ways of doing business.

11.4 Conclusion

Leadership comes in many forms and many styles. The environmental leadership examples presented in this book do not purport to hold up any one company as having arrived at a perfect state of sustainability. But, in their journey toward more sustainable practices, they have successfully adopted some of the new tools and principles of environmental management. In following this path, these leadership companies are finding value-creation opportunities for themselves and their stakeholders—the hallmark of good business practices.

Leadership, environmental ethics, transforming business strategies, creating value for shareholders and stakeholders alike—all are attributes of those companies exhibiting best-in-class characteristics for sustaining environmental management.

INFORMATION SOURCES

Environment-Related Websites

The following websites contain information relevant to the broad issues of environmental management and sustainability:

www.iso.ch	Official site for the ISO Central Secretariat
www.un.org/dpcsd/dsd	U.N. indicators for sustainable development
www.astm.org	American Society for Testing & Materials
web.ansi.org	American National Standards Institute
web.ansi.org/public/ ISO14000	ANSI ISO 14000 general information
www.ISO14000.net	GETF ISO 14000 general information
www.gov/envirosense/ partners/iso	U.S. EPA ISO 14000 general information
web.ansi.org/rooms/ room_33/public	TC 207 SC 4 (EPE) official site
www.cutter.com	Cutter Information Corporation
www.clay.net	Accessing environmental resources

Organizational Sources

Following you will find many of the organizations that provide information on ISO 14000, ISO 9000, and related standards and environmental management concepts and principles. The actual ISO 14000 series of standards may be purchased directly from either ISO, ANSI, ASQC, or ASTM.

INFORMATION SOURCES

International Organization for Standardization

The International Organization for Standardization (ISO) is a worldwide non-government federation of national standards bodies from more than 100 countries. ISO was founded in 1947 with the mission of promoting the development of standardization. ISO's work results in international agreements that are published as international standards.

> The International Organization for Standardization
> 1, rue de Varembe
> Case postale 50
> CH-1211 Geneva 20, Switzerland
> Telephone: +41-22-749-0111
> Fax: +41-22-733-3430
> E-mail: central@isocs.iso.ch

American National Standards Institute

The American National Standards Institute (ANSI) is a nonprofit organization that adopts U.S. standards and coordinates standard development activity in the United States. ANSI is the official U.S. representative to ISO.

> The American National Standards Institute
> 11 West 42nd Street
> New York, NY 10036
> Telephone: (212) 642-4900
> Fax: (212) 398-0023
> E-mail: info@ansi.org

The American Society for Quality

The American Society for Quality (ASQ) is a professional nonprofit organization that addresses quality management and environmental management standardization issues and educational services through its numerous committees. ASQ serves as the U.S. administrator for SubTAGs 1 and 2.

The American Society for Quality
611 East Wisconsin Avenue
P.O. Box 3005
Milwaukee, WI 53201
Telephone: (414) 272-8575; (800) 248-1946
Fax: (414) 272-1734

The American Society for Testing & Materials

The American Society for Testing & Materials (ASTM) is a nonprofit organization that prepares standards for use in industry and commerce. For example, ASTM has prepared standards for environmental site assessments, environmental compliance auditing and environmental management systems. ASTM serves as an administrator to the U.S. TAG.

The American Society for Testing & Materials
100 Barr Harbor Drive
West Conshohocken, PA 19428-2959
Telephone: (610) 832-9585
Fax: (610) 832-9555

U.S. Subtag I Sanctioned ISO 14001 Interpretation Guidance

The U.S. Subtag 1 has established a formal process to clarify questions and to present the official U.S. Subtag 1 consensus interpretation of the words of ISO 14001. The subtag has established a Drafting Group to answer questions submitted in writing. The contact provided here can provide details on the procedures for submitting questions.

Patricia Kopp
611 East Wisconsin Avenue
P.O. Box 3005
Milwaukee, Wisconsin 53201-3005
Telephone: (414) 272-8575
Fax: (414) 272-1734

NSF International

NSF International is a U.S. standards development, research, and educational organization. NSF developed an Environmental Management System standard, NSF 110, prior to the availability of ISO 14001. NSF provides registration services, publications, and training.

> NSF International
> 3475 Plymouth Road
> P.O. Box 130140
> Ann Arbor, MI 48113
> Telephone: (313) 769-8010; (800) 673-6275
> Fax: (313) 769-0109

Global Environment & Technology Foundation

The Global Environment & Technology Foundation (GETF) was founded "To raise competitiveness, improve environmental protection, and encourage an environmental ethic by assisting public and private sector organizations to leverage the ISO 14000 standards." GETF has a collaborative partnership with ANSI to develop and maintain a state-of-the-art web site (ISO 14000 Integrated Solutions—"IIS On-Line") to provide comprehensive information to those interested in ISO 1400.

> Global Environment & Technology Foundation
> 7010 Little River Turnpike
> Suite 300
> Annandale, VA 22003-3241
> Telephone: (703) 750-6401
> Fax: (703) 750-6506

Global Environmental Management Initiative

The Global Environmental Management Initiative (GEMI) is a nongovernmental organization that describes itself as "business helping business achieve environmental, health and safety excellence." The organization publishes numerous member-generated publications, such as "Benchmarking: The Primer," "ISO 14001 Environmental Management System: Self Assessment Checklist," "Total Quality Environmental Management: The Primer," and others.

GEMI
1090 Vermont Avenue, N.W., 3rd Floor
Washington, D.C. 20005
Telephone: (202) 296-7449
Fax: (202) 296-7442
E-mail: GEMI@worldweb.net

National Association for Environmental Management

The National Association for Environmental Management (NAEM) was organized to advance and promote environmental management principles, including support for the implementation of standards and guidelines. It commonly holds annual environmental management conferences and workshops.

National Association For Environmental Management
2025 Eye Street
Suite 1126
Washington, D.C. 20006
Telephone: (202) 986-6616; (800) 391-NAEM
Fax: (202) 530-4408

CEEM Information Services

CEEM Information Services provides ISO 14000 information through its monthly newsletter, *International Environmental Systems Update*, and several recent comprehensive books. CEEM also offers ISO 14000 training courses.

CEEM Information Services
10521 Braddock Road
Fairfax, VA 22032-2236
Telephone: (703) 250-5900; (800) 745-5565
Fax: (703) 250-4117

INFORMATION SOURCES

Cutter Information Corporation

Cutter Information Corporation publishes *Business and the Environment* and *ISO 14000 Update*.

> Cutter Information Corp.
> 37 Broadway, Suite 1
> Arlington, MA 02174-5552
> Telephone: (781) 641-5125; (800) 964-5125
> Fax: (781) 648-1950

Environment Watch Western Europe

Environment Watch provides news and analysis for business and policy professionals on environmental affairs in the European Union.

> Environment Watch Western Europe
> Boulevard Charlemagne 26
> 10000 Brussels, Belgium
> Telephone: +32 2 230 8978
> Fax: +32 2 230 8558
> Telephone (U.S.): (617) 641-5125
> Fax (U.S.): (617) 648-1950
> E-mail: tcarritt@gn.apc.org

ENVIRONMENTAL TERMS AND DEFINITIONS

The following terms are commonly used in environmental management. Do note that some of these terms have formal definitions within the ISO 14000 standards. For a copy of the standards, contact your national standards body.

accreditation A formal recognition of the capability and competence of an organization to conduct registration or certification activities related to ISO standards or other types of conformity assessments.

audit A systematic, documented, periodic, objective assessment of operations or practices in comparison to stated requirements. In the case of ISO EMS audits, the stated requirement is the EMS standard ISO 14001. In the case of regulatory compliance audits, the requirements are generally the applicable state, local, and federal environmental laws and regulations.

benchmarking The technique of comparing an organization, function, or process to other best in class organizations with the intent of making quality or performance improvements.

certification Verifying or attesting that a process or system conforms to specified requirements. The term is generally synonymous with **registration** in addressing ISO 14001 EMS certifications.

continual improvement The systematic process of improving a process, function, operation, or entire organization, especially by utilizing the principles and approaches embodied in TQM. In the context of EMS, the focus is on the continual improvement of an organization's environmental management system.

corrective action Any action taken to eliminate a nonconformance or deficiency in a system, especially addressing the root cause of that nonconformance.

environmental aspect   Any element of an organization or its activities or products that has the potential to interact positively or negatively with the environment.

Environmental Management System   A system for addressing the environmental policies, objectives, procedures, principles, authority, responsibility, accountability and implementation of an organization's means for managing its environmental affairs.

environmental policy   An organization's statement of environmental principles, which serves as the basis for setting performance goals and environmental targets and objectives.

guideline   Generally a suggested practice whose use and application is discretionary, even in the context of complying with a standard.

ISO 9000   The Quality Management System standards established by the International Organization for Standardization (ISO).

ISO 14000   The Environmental Management System series of standards established by the International Organization for Standardization (ISO).

management system   A system for addressing the policies, objectives, principles, authority, responsibilities, accountability, and implementation plan of an organization.

organization   In ISO terms, *organization* refers to any privately held or public company (profit or nonprofit), institution, or enterprise (including cooperatives) that has its own administration and governance.

prevention of pollution   A term specific to the ISO 14000 standards that can include recycling, treatment, process changes, control mechanisms, material substitutions, or the more efficient use of resources. A term in common usage, *pollution prevention,* generally implies a narrower application of early-stage steps (process redesign, for instance) taken to prevent or reduce the sources of waste generation. Prevention of pollution then includes the activity of pollution prevention as one of its options.

quality   The features and characteristics of a product or service that relate to its ability to conform to or meet the stated or implied requirements.

registrar   A recognized and accredited third-party organization that conducts independent auditing and certification of a company's quality management system or environmental management system.

registration   The procedure whereby a qualified registrar verifies an organization's conformance to the requirements of ISO 9000 or ISO 14000. In the United States, this term is generally synonymous with the term **certi-fication** for EMS purposes.

self-assessment Assessments of any efforts, activities, systems, and so forth when the assessors are not independent of those items or practices under evaluation.

stakeholder Any individuals, parties or groups that have a vested interest in the environmental aspects of an organization, its operations, and its products. Stakeholders may include stockholders, employees, the community, customers, suppliers, contractors, and interested parties, such as conservation and environmental advocacy groups.

standard A protocol established by a recognized authority as a rule or requirement.

supplier An individual or organization that furnishes products or services to another in accordance with an agreement between those two parties.

sustainable development Development that provides social, economic, and environmental benefits in the long term, taking regard of the needs of living and future generations.

targets and objectives *Objectives* are overall goals set by the organization for itself, whereas *targets* are detailed performance requirements with time schedules that arise from the objectives and allow the objectives to be achieved.

third party Any individuals, groups, or organizations fully independent of the subject organization. A consulting environmental auditing firm or an ISO 14000 registrar are examples of third parties.

Total Quality Management (TQM) A process for committing to, and focusing on, quality management principles, including the continuous improvement of products and services.

COMMONLY USED
ABBREVIATIONS AND ACRONYMS

ANSI	American National Standards Institute
ASQC	American Society for Quality Control
ASTM	American Society for Testing and Materials
BSI	British Standards Institute
BVQI	Bureau Veritas Quality International Ltd.
CAG	Chairman's Advisory Group (TAG)
CASCO	Committee on Conformity Assessment (ISO)
CD	Committee Draft
CEN	Comite Europeen de Normalisation
CMA	Chemical Manufacturers Association
CSI	Common Sense Initiative (U.S. EPA)
DfD	Design for Disassembly
DfE	Design for the Environment
DIS	Draft International Standard
ELP	Environmental Leadership Program (U.S. EPA)
EMAR	Eco-Management and Audit Regulation (E.U.)
EMAS	Eco-Management and Auditing Scheme (E.U.)
EMI	Environmental management indicator (management area)
EMIS	Environmental Management Information System
EMS	Environmental Management System
EPA	Environmental Protection Agency (U.S.)
EPE	Environmental performance evaluation
EPI	Environmental performance indicator (operational area)
ERP	Enterprise Resource Planning
EU	European Union
FDIS	Final Draft International Standard
ICC	International Chamber of Commerce

ISO	International Organization for Standardization
IT	Information technology
LCA	Life-Cycle Assessment
LCM	Life-Cycle Management
MSDS	Material safety data sheet
NAFTA	North American Free Trade Agreement
NIST	National Institute of Standards and Technology (U.S. Department of Commerce)
NGO	Nongovernmental organization
OEM	Original equipment manufacturer
OSHA	U.S. Occupational Safety and Health Administration
PCSD	President's Council on Sustainable Development
PERI	Public Environmental Reporting Initiative
P2	Pollution prevention
PPMs	Process and production methods
QMS	Quality management system
RAB	Registrar Accreditation Board
SAGE	Strategic Advisory Group on Environment
SC	Subcommittee (TC 207)
SI	Systems integration
SIC	Standard Industrial Classification Code (U.S.)
SME	Small or medium enterprises
ST	SubTAG (U.S. TAG)
TAG	Technical Advisory Group (TAG)
TBT	Technical barriers to trade
TC	Technical Committee
TG	Task Group
TMB	Technical Management Board (ISO)
TQEM	Total Quality Environmental Management
TQM	Total Quality Management
TRI	Toxic Release Inventory (SARA Title III)
UNCED	United Nations Conference on the Environment and Development
WD	Working Draft
WG	Working Group
WTO	World Trade Organization
XL	Project Excellence and Leadership (U.S. EPA)

D

THE RIO DECLARATION ON ENVIRONMENT AND DEVELOPMENT

The United Nations Conference on Environment and Development, having met at Rio de Janeiro from 3 to 14 June 1992, reaffirming the Declaration of the United Nations Conference on the Human Environment, adopted at Stockholm on 16 June 1972, and seeking to build upon it, with the goal of establishing a new and equitable global partnership through the creation of new levels of cooperation among States, key sectors of societies and people, working towards international agreements which respect the interests of all and protect the integrity of the global environmental and developmental system, recognizing the integral and interdependent nature of the Earth, our home, proclaims that:

Principle 1

Human beings are at the center of concerns for sustainable development. They are entitled to a healthy and productive life in harmony with nature.

Principle 2

States have, in accordance with the Charter of the United Nations and the principles of international law, the sovereign right to exploit their own resources pursuant to their own environmental and developmental policies, and the responsibility to ensure that activities within their jurisdiction or control do not cause damage to the environment of other States or of areas beyond the limits of national jurisdiction.

Principle 3

The right to development must be fulfilled so as to equitably meet developmental and environmental needs of present and future generations.

Principle 4

In order to achieve sustainable development, environmental protection shall constitute an integral part of the development process and cannot be considered in isolation from it.

Principle 5

All States and all people shall cooperate in the essential task of eradicating poverty as an indispensable requirement for sustainable development, in order to decrease the disparities in standards of living and better meet the needs of the majority of the people of the world.

Principle 6

The special situation and needs of developing countries, particularly the least developed and those most environmentally vulnerable, shall be given special priority. International actions in the field of environment and development should also address the interests and needs of all countries.

Principle 7

States shall cooperate in a spirit of global partnership to conserve, protect and restore the health and integrity of the Earth's ecosystem. In view of the different contributions to global environmental degradation, States have common but differentiated responsibilities. The developed countries acknowledge the responsibility that they bear in the international pursuit of sustainable development in view of the pressures their societies place on the global environment and of the technologies and financial resources they command.

Principle 8

To achieve sustainable development and a higher quality of life for all people, States should reduce and eliminate unsustainable patterns of production and consumption and promote appropriate demographic policies.

Principle 9

States should cooperate to strengthen endogenous capacity-building for sustainable development by improving scientific understanding through exchanges of scientific and technological knowledge, and by enhancing the development, adaptation, diffusion and transfer of technologies, including new and innovative technologies.

Principle 10

Environmental issues are best handled with the participation of all concerned citizens, at the relevant level. At the national level, each individual shall have appropriate access to information concerning the environment that is held by public authorities, including information on hazardous materials and activities in their communities, and the opportunity to participate in decision-making processes. States shall facilitate and encourage public awareness and participation by making information widely available. Effective access to judicial and administrative proceedings, including redress and remedy, shall be provided.

Principle 11

States shall enact effective environmental legislation. Environmental standards, management objectives and priorities should reflect the environmental and developmental context to which they apply. Standards applied by some countries can be inappropriate and of unwarranted economic and social cost to other countries, in particular developing countries.

Principle 12

States should cooperate to promote a supportive and open international economic system that would lead to economic growth and sustainable development in all countries, to better address the problems of environmental degradation. Trade policy measures for environmental purposes should not constitute a means of arbitrary or unjustifiable discrimination or a disguised restriction on international trade. Unilateral actions to deal with environmental challenges outside the jurisdiction of the importing country should be avoided. Environmental measures addressing transboundary or global environmental problems should, as far as possible, be based on an international consensus.

Principle 13

States shall develop national law regarding liability and compensation for the victims of pollution and other environmental damage. States shall also cooperate in an expeditious and more determined manner to develop further international law regarding liability and compensation for adverse effects of environmental damage caused by activities within their jurisdiction or control to areas beyond their jurisdiction.

Principle 14

States should effectively cooperate to discourage or prevent the relocation and transfer to other States of any activities and substances that cause severe environmental degradation or are found to be harmful to human health.

Principle 15

In order to protect the environment, the precautionary approach shall be widely applied by States according to their capabilities. Where there are threats of serious or irreversible damage, lack of full scientific certainty shall not be used as a reason for postponing cost-effective measures to prevent environmental degradation.

Principle 16

National authorities should endeavor to promote the internalization of environmental costs and the use of economic instruments, taking into account the approach that the polluter should, in principle, bear the cost of pollution, with due regard to the public interest and without distorting international trade and investment.

Principle 17

Environmental impact assessment, as a national instrument, shall be undertaken for proposed activities that are likely to have a significant adverse impact on the environment and are subject to a decision of a competent national authority.

Principle 18

States shall immediately notify other States of any natural disasters or other emergencies that are likely to produce sudden harmful effects on the environment of those States. Every effort shall be made by the international community to help States so afflicted.

Principle 19

States shall provide prior and timely notification and relevant information to potentially affected States on activities that can have a significant adverse transboundary environmental effect and shall consult with those States at an early stage and in good faith.

Principle 20

Women have a vital role in environmental management and development. Their full participation is therefore essential to achieve sustainable development.

Principle 21

The creativity, ideals and courage of the youth of the world should be mobilized to forge a global partnership in order to achieve sustainable development and ensure a better future for all.

Principle 22

Indigenous people and their communities, and other local communities, have a vital role in environmental management and development because of their knowledge and traditional practices. States should recognize and duly support their identity, culture and interest and enable their effective participation in the achievement of sustainable development.

Principle 23

The environment and natural resources of people under oppression, domination and occupation shall be protected.

Principle 24

Warfare is inherently destructive of sustainable development. States shall therefore respect international law providing protection for the environment in times of armed conflict and cooperate in its future development, as necessary.

Principle 25

Peace, development and environmental protection are interdependent and indivisible.

Principle 26

States shall resolve all their environmental disputes peacefully and by appropriate means in accordance with the Charter of the United Nations.

Principle 27

States and people shall cooperate in good faith and in a spirit of partnership in the fulfillment of the principles embodied in this Declaration and in the further development of international law in the field of sustainable development.

NOTES

Chapter 1

1. For a thorough discussion of sustainable development see Schmidheiny (1992).
2. *Product stewardship* is the term generally applied to initiatives aimed at minimizing pollution during manufacturing, packaging, use, and disposal of a product. A subset of product stewardship is *design for the environment*, which means developing a product in such a manner that the product will be easier to reuse, recycle, or recover. Product stewardship is a key component of sustainable production.

Chapter 4

1. ISO 14000 refers to the series of environmental management–related standards being developed by ISO Technical Committee 207. "ISO 14001:1996—Environmental management systems—Specifications with guidance for use" and "ISO 14004:1996—Environmental management systems—General guidelines on principles, systems and supporting techniques" were published in the fall of 1996 and provide the bases for development of an EMS. Other standards in the series are in various stages of development and provide guidance on EMS auditing (ISO 14010, 14011, and 14012; all published in fall 1996), environmental labeling (ISO 14020s), environmental performance evaluation (ISO 14031), and life-cycle analysis (ISO 14040s). ISO 14001 is the only standard in the series against which a company can be certified; all other standards are for guidance.

The European Commission (EU) published the Eco-Management and Audit Regulation (EMAR) in the summer of 1993 to promote continuous environmental performance improvement in companies that have industrial operations in the EU countries. The Eco-Management and Audit Scheme (EMAS) is an accompanying document which provides the systems approach that is embodied in EMAR.

Chapter 5

1. A *gap analysis* is nothing more than a comparison of your procedures to those required to meet the certification requirements of ISO 14001. In the more general sense, an initial review results in an understanding of your current state of the art relative to environmental management and environmental performance.

Chapter 9

1. Detailed information on the index, including how to make each calculation, is available at the company's website: http://www.nortel.com/cool/environ/epi.

Chapter 11

1. An article on values-based environmental management is scheduled for 1998 publication in the *Journal of Strategic Environmental Management.*

REFERENCES

AICPA. *Statement of Position 96-1, Environmental Remediation Liabilities.* New York: American Institute of Certified Public Accountants, 1996.

ANSI/ISO. "Environmental Management Systems—Specification with Guideline for Use." ANSI/ISO Standard 14001—1996. New York/Geneva, 1996a.

ANSI/ISO. "Environmental Management Systems—General Guidelines on Principles, Systems and Supporting Techniques." ANSI/ISO Standard 14004—1996. New York/Geneva, 1996b.

Blumberg, Jerald, Korsvold, Åge, and Blum, George. *Environmental Performance and Shareholder Value.* Geneva: World Business Council for Sustainable Development, 1997.

Deloitte Touche Tohmatsu International, International Institute for Sustainable Development, and SustainAbility. *Coming Clean: Corporate Environmental Reporting, Opening Up for Sustainable Development.* London: Deloitte Touche Tohmatsu, 1993.

Ditz, Daryl, Ranganathan, Janet, and Banks, R. Darryl, eds. *Green Ledgers: Case Studies in Corporate Environmental Accounting.* World Resources Institute, May 1995.

Feldman, Stanley J., Soyka, Peter A., and Ameer, Paul. "Does Improving a Firm's Environmental Management System and Environmental Performance Result in a Higher Stock Price?" ICF Kaiser International, November, 1996.

GEMI. *Benchmarking: The Primer. Benchmarking for Continuous Environmental Improvement.* Washington, D.C.: Global Environmental Management Initiative, 1994.

Hart, Stuart L., "Beyond Greening: Strategies For A Sustainable World." *Harvard Business Review,* January–February, 1997.

REFERENCES

Hart, Stuart L., and Ahuje, Gautam. "Does It Pay to Be Green? An Empirical Examination of the Relationship between Emission Reduction and Firm Performance." *Business Strategy and the Environment,* 1996.

ISO. "Life Cycle Assessment—Principles and Framework." ISO Standard 14040—1997. Geneva, 1997.

ISO. "Environmental Management—Environmental Performance Evaluation—Guidelines." ISO Draft International Standard 14031. Geneva, 1998

Jones, Patricia, and Kahaner, Larry. *Say It and Live It: The 50 Corporate Mission Statements That Hit the Mark.* New York: Currency Doubleday, 1995.

Kaplan, Robert S., and Norton, David. *Translating Strategy into Action: The Balanced Scorecard.* Cambridge, Mass.: Harvard Business School Press, 1996.

Kelly, Marjorie. "Capitalism Grows Up." *Business Ethics,* January–February, 1995.

KPMG. "1996 Canadian Environmental Management Survey." KPMG Canada, 1996.

KPMG Bohlins Environmental Advisors and the International Institute for Industrial Environmental Economics. *International Survey of Environmental Reporting 1996.* Lund University, Sweden, March 1997.

Lober, Douglas J. "What Makes Environmental Reports Effective: Current Trends in Corporate Reporting. *Corporate Environmental Strategy,* Winter 1997.

Lober, Douglas J., Bynum, David, Campbell, Elizabeth, and Jacques, Mary. "The 100 Plus Corporate Environmental Report Study: A Survey of an Evolving Environmental Tool." *Business Strategy and the Environment,* 6:57–73, 1997.

Magretta, Joan. "Growth through Global Sustainability: An Interview with Monsanto's CEO, Robert B. Shapiro." *Harvard Business Review,* January–February, 1997.

NSF International. *Environmental Management Systems: An Implementation Guide for Small and Medium-Sized Organizations.* Ann Arbor, Mich., November 1996.

Porter, Michael E., and van der Linde, Claas. "Green and Competitive: Ending the Stalemate." *Harvard Business Review,* September–October, 1995.

REFERENCES

President's Council on Sustainable Development. *Sustainable America: A New Consensus for Prosperity, Opportunity and a Healthy Environment.* Washington, D.C., February 1996.

Sasseville, D. R., Wilson, W. G., and Lawson, R. *The ISO 14000 Answer Book: Environmental Management for the World Market.* New York: John Wiley & Sons, 1997.

Schmidheiny, Stephan, with the Business Council for Sustainable Development. *Changing Course: A Global Business Perspective on Development and the Environment.* Cambridge, Mass.: MIT Press, 1992.

USA Today. "Passively Green." USA Snapshots, January 30, 1997.

U.S. Department of Justice. "Factors in Decisions on Criminal Prosecutions for Environmental Violations in the Context of Significant Voluntary Compliance Efforts by the Violator." Washington, D.C., July 1991.

U.S. Environmental Protection Agency. *An Introduction to Environmental Accounting as a Business Management Tool: Key Concepts and Terms.* EPA 742-R-95-001. Washington, D.C.: Office of Pollution Prevention and Toxics, June 1995.

U.S. Environmental Protection Agency. "Incentives for Self-Policing: Discovery, Disclosure, Correction and Prevention of Violations." U.S. EPA Final Audit Policy. *Federal Register,* December 22, 1995.

Wever, Grace H. *Strategic Environmental Management: Using TQEM and ISO 14000 for Competitive Advantage.* New York: John Wiley & Sons, 1996.

World Commission on Environment and Development. *Our Common Future.* New York: Oxford University Press, 1987.

Yosie, Terry F., and Herbst, Timothy D. *Corporate Environmental, Health and Safety Practices in Transition: Management System Responses to Changing Public Expectations, Regulatory Requirements and Incentives.* Washington, D.C.: Global Environmental Management Initiative, September 1996.

INDEX

INDEX

INDEX

INDEX

INDEX

INDEX

INDEX

INDEX

INDEX